CLIMATE CHANGE
in
HUMAN HISTORY

How a changing climate drove human
evolution and the rise of civilization

CLIMATE CHANGE

in

HUMAN HISTORY

How a changing climate drove human
evolution and the rise of civilization

FRANCIS H. CHAPELLE

DEFIANCE PRESS
& PUBLISHING

Climate Change in Human History

Printed in the United States of America

10 9 8 7 6 5 4 3 2 1

DEFIANCE PRESS
& PUBLISHING

ISBN-13: 978-1-955937-99-3 (Paperback)
ISBN-13: 978-1-955937-98-6 (eBook)
ISBN-13: 978-1-959677-00-0 (Hardcover

Published by Defiance Press & Publishing, LLC

Bulk orders of this book may be obtained by contacting Defiance Press & Publishing, LLC. www.defiancepress.com.

Public Relations Dept. – Defiance Press & Publishing, LLC
281-581-9300
pr@defiancepress.com

Defiance Press & Publishing, LLC
281-581-9300
info@defiancepress.com

Cover photo credit: Walid Ahmad

TABLE OF CONTENTS

The earth's climate, as far back in the history of the earth that we can see, has never been constant. Rather, warming trends have always alternated with subsequent cooling trends throughout the history of the earth. These periodic climate reversals are, and have always been, a major stress for life on earth, and thus a driving force for evolutionary and social change for humans.

The Medieval Warm Period came to an end in 1257 CE when the Samalas volcano in Indonesia exploded, sending sulfur aerosols into the stratosphere and causing the atmosphere to suddenly cool. Crops in England failed in 1258 CE, causing a famine in which 15,000 people died in London alone.

Climate change began when the earth first acquired a permanent atmosphere four billion years ago. At first, earth's atmospheric temperatures reflected the coexistence of liquid water and water vaper. Something changed 2.42 billion years ago, and the planet froze into a "snowball earth."

A warming trend five million years ago in East Africa turned the lush jungles into a dry savannah, creating environmental stresses that shaped the evolution of humanity.

How heat-adapted humans living in Siberia 20,000 years ago during the peak of the last ice age managed to survive and thrive.

How Milutin Milanković deduced that changes in the earth's orbit, axial tilt, and rotational wobble combine to cause periodic ice ages.

How a warming trend that began 10,000 years ago led to the invention of agriculture.

How a cooling climate that commenced about 1,200 BCE led to the collapse of the Mycenaean, Babylonian, and Hittite civilizations.

How the Roman Warm Period (300 BCE to 400 CE) facilitated the rise of Rome, and how the cooling trend of the Little Antique Ice Age (400-750 CE) contributed to Rome's collapse.

PREFACE

CLIMATE CHANGE IS WIDELY CONSIDERED to be the most serious environmental issue humanity faces in the twenty-first century, and it is. But climate change is nothing new in human history, and it is something that humans and proto-humans have been dealing with (more or less successfully) for at least five million years.

Ten million years ago, dense tropical jungles covered East Africa, the cradle of humanity, supporting hundreds of species of monkeys and apes. Beginning about nine million years ago, however, the warm moist climate began to change. Specifically, over the next four million years, the climate warmed further and began to dry out. Gradually, the lush jungles retreated into the few river valleys still meandering through the landscape. The uplands surrounding the river valleys dried out, replaced by arid and semi-arid plains and savannahs. The ancestors of modern chimpanzees, bonobos, and gorillas followed the retreating jungles into river valleys and foggy mountain ranges. Because those moist environments were shrinking steadily, competition between apes and monkeys for available space and food resources became increasingly severe. For that reason, the ancestors of modern humans moved tentatively into the surrounding dry savannahs and began exploiting a new ecological niche that involved gathering seeds, nuts, and tuber-bearing plants now growing on the plains. Crucially, they gathered those food resources in the heat of the day when the fearsome African predators—the nocturnal leopards, lions, and hyenas—were comparatively inactive. Within a million years, these proto-humans were fully bipedal, had largely lost their dense fur, and cooled themselves under the hot sun by perspiring.

The beginnings of humanity, in other words, can be traced directly to climate change.

$$\Longleftrightarrow$$

As far back in earth's history that we can see, the climate has never been constant. Rather, warming trends have always alternated with subsequent cooling trends. The change from warming to cooling, or from cooling to warming, is known as a *climate reversal*, and each occurrence profoundly affects earth's ecosystems and the human societies depending on those ecosystems. There have been at least four major climate reversals in written human history alone.

The Bronze Age in the Middle East, which began about 3300 BCE, was characterized by a warm climate with fairly predictable rainfall. Those favorable climatic conditions led to the invention and spread of agriculture, which led to the rise of cities and civilization. Many of those civilizations collapsed rather suddenly around 1200 BCE when a cooling climate and decreased rainfall caused an agricultural crisis throughout the Mediterranean basin that was followed by famines and epidemics. The great Mycenaean, Minoan, Babylonian, Canaanite, Cypriot, and Hittite civilizations of the Late Bronze Age collapsed. The Egyptian civilization also teetered on the brink of annihilation when desperate and probably starving "Sea Peoples" invaded. The Egyptians held on, the only Mediterranean civilization to survive the upheavals accompanying climate reversal that ended the Late Bronze Age.

Another climate reversal occurred at the end of what is known as the Roman Warm Period (300 BCE to 400 CE), a time characterized by generally warm temperatures around the Mediterranean basin with predictable rainfall, good agricultural production, and growing human populations. When a sudden cooling trend known as the "Late Antique Little Ice Age" set in about 400 CE, Germanic barbarians from the east crossed the Rhine River into the Roman Empire, possibly because the Rhine River froze solid in the winter of 406 CE. When these barbarians sacked Rome in 410 CE, it marked the beginning of the end for the Western Roman Empire.

A third climate reversal occurred at the end of the Medieval Warm Period (750 – 1300 CE), a time of rising temperatures, increased agricultural production, and increasing human populations in Europe. That warming period ended in 1300 CE when another abrupt cooling trend, probably triggered by a series of exploding volcanos around the Pacific Rim, caused a massive famine in Europe in which tens of thousands of people starved to death. That cooling trend, known as the "Little Ice Age" lasted until about 1860 CE, initiating the "Modern Warm Time," which we are presently experiencing.

The historical pattern is clear. Warming climate trends initially benefit people (civilizations thrive and populations increase), only to be reversed when something happens to initiate a cooling trend (massive volcanic explosions, variations in the earth's orbital dynamics, decreasing solar radiation output, changes in ocean current/atmospheric dynamics). The implications for us in the twenty-first century are obvious. The Modern Warm Time has been in place since the end of the Little Ice Ages in 1860 CE. That warming trend has been accelerated by the combustion of fossil fuels and increasing carbon dioxide concentrations in the atmosphere that accompanied the Industrial Revolution. As was the case in the Middle Bronze Age, the Roman Warm Period, and the Medieval Warm Period, the human population has grown enormously during the Modern Warm Time. But warming trends, for as far back in earth's history as we can see, are always punctuated by subsequent cooling trends. The threats of global warming (sea level rise, species extinctions, storm intensity, desertization) have been recognized since the 1980s. But the much greater threat of a warm-to-cool climate reversal (agricultural collapse, famine, disease, political instability) is not widely recognized outside of scholarly, historical, and climatological circles.

The purpose of this book is to show how climate change has affected the evolution of our hominin ancestors over the last five million years, how the fully modern humans who emerged 100,000 years ago dealt with recurrent cycles of warming and cooling (i.e. the ice ages), how a warming trend 10,000 years ago ended the last ice age and led to the agricultural revolution, how recurrent warming trends allowed civilizations to rise, and how cooling trends sometimes contributed to their demise. To achieve these ends, this book reviews the vast array of solar, orbital, tectonic, oceanic, and atmospheric processes that combine to cause periodic climate reversals. Finally, this book shows how those reversals have affected natural ecosystems and human societies through time.

Our modern civilization is threatened by climate change in the same ways that helped build and then destroy the Bronze Age and Roman civilizations. Part of this threat, of course, comes from global warming, which has contributed mightily to human population growth in the twentieth and twenty-first centuries. Equally dangerous, however, is something that few people today are aware of.

The inevitability of eventual global cooling.

CHAPTER 1
Climate Reversals

IN 1257 CE, EUROPE was in the Medieval Warm Period with temperatures as warm as those today. The benevolent weather was a boon to agriculture, with grapes actually grown in northern England. The winter of 1257/58 CE was especially warm, leading a contemporary chronicler to remark:[1]

> ....*frost barely lasted for more than two days. In January, violets could be observed, and strawberries and apple trees were in blossom.*

That warmth, however, was short lived. As the spring turned to summer, the weather cooled dramatically, thick clouds filled the skies, and it rained incessantly. Another chronicler described the unusual weather like this:[2]

> *What, then, shall I say about the fruits of the earth that year, when the weather was so remarkably unseasonable that the warmth of the Sun was hardly able, even a little, to reach the earth, and the fruits of that year could barely attain maturity, if at all? For so great a thickness of clouds covered the sky throughout that whole summer that hardly anyone could tell whether it was summer or autumn. The hay, drenched incessantly by strong rains that year, was unable to dry out, because it could not collect the warmth of the Sun on account of the thickness of the clouds.*

It wasn't just the hay crop that was ruined. Throughout most of Europe and Britain, the cool temperatures and excessive summer rain caused widespread crop failures that were inevitably followed by a famine. England was particularly hard hit. Without their harvest, peasants in the countryside began starving, and, not knowing where else to turn, they converged on London hoping to find food. That winter, as many as 15,000 people starved to death in London alone, thousands of which were buried in huge communal graves.[3] Europe was not alone in suffering from famine between 1257 and 1260 CE. Japan also experienced a devastating famine during that same time frame.[4]

⇔

Climate can be defined generally as weather conditions experienced in a particular area (the entire earth, a country, a city) over a defined time period (a year, a century, a millennia). Those "weather conditions" are described by one or more measureable parameters such as temperature, humidity, rainfall, snowfall, etc. By that definition, the "climate" of Europe during the summer of 1258 certainly turned markedly cooler and wetter than it had been over the past century.

Beginning about 750 CE, Europe's climate exited the relatively cold period, known as the Late Antique Little Ice Age (400-750 CE) that dominated the Dark Ages, and began a gradual warming trend that lasted until 1300 CE. That warming trend was reversed in the summer and fall of 1258 CE when suddenly the weather turned much cooler, a change that lasted for about ten years.[5] This is an example of a *climate reversal*: a sudden and rapid change between a warm, benevolent weather pattern to one cooler and less favorable for agriculture.

What could possibly explain this sudden change? The climate reversal that struck Europe in 1258 CE coincided with a massive eruption of a volcano now known as Samalas in Indonesia.[1] That eruption, the largest that has occurred in the last 7,000 years, ejected as much as 158 million tons of sulfur dioxide into the stratosphere. The sulfur dioxide reacted chemically with atmospheric gases to produce sulfuric acid aerosols that circled the globe in mere weeks. Those aerosols immediately began to reflect solar radiation out into space and away from the earth. Within months of the eruption, the earth's climate cooled, an effect that persisted for several years until the aerosols finally dispersed.

It's tempting to conclude, therefore, that the Samalas eruption of 1257 CE "caused" the great famine of 1258-1260 CE. The eruption and the resulting short-term cooling trend certainly contributed to the famine, but ironically, so did the warming trend of the Medieval Warm Period (MWP). Beginning around 750 CE, the gradual warming trend aided agricultural productivity in Europe. The increased availability of food, in turn, allowed the population to grow. The British Isles, for example, had a total population of about half a million people in 650 CE prior to the MWP.[6] At the height of the MWP, the total population of the British Isles had risen to between five and seven million people.[6] By the time of the Samalas eruption in 1257 CE, the population was so large that any interruption in agricultural productivity would inevitably cause food shortages. The result was a horrible famine.[3,4,5] While the cooling trend caused by the Samalas eruption certainly contributed to the famine, so did the warming trend of the MWP that allowed Europe's population to grow so rapidly.

The historical lesson of the 1258 CE famine is that the threat of climate change to humans is not just global warming (as many people today think). The larger threat is a warming trend (generally favorable to human societies) that reverses and the climate suddenly and unexpectedly cools. We are presently in a period of global warming that began when the earth's climate emerged from the Little Ice Age in 1860 CE. During this period of global warming, the world's human population increased from about 1.2 billion people in 1860 CE to almost eight billion people today. That's about the same percentage population increase that occurred in the British Iles during the Medieval Warm Period.

What will happen when the next climate reversal occurs?

⇔

The Earth's climate has always been in a state of flux, with warming trends constantly alternating with cooling trends over a variety of different time scales. Just how the temperature of the earth's oceans have changed over the last 550 million years is indicated by $^{18}O/^{16}O$ ratios in the shells of marine organisms (Figure 1.1).

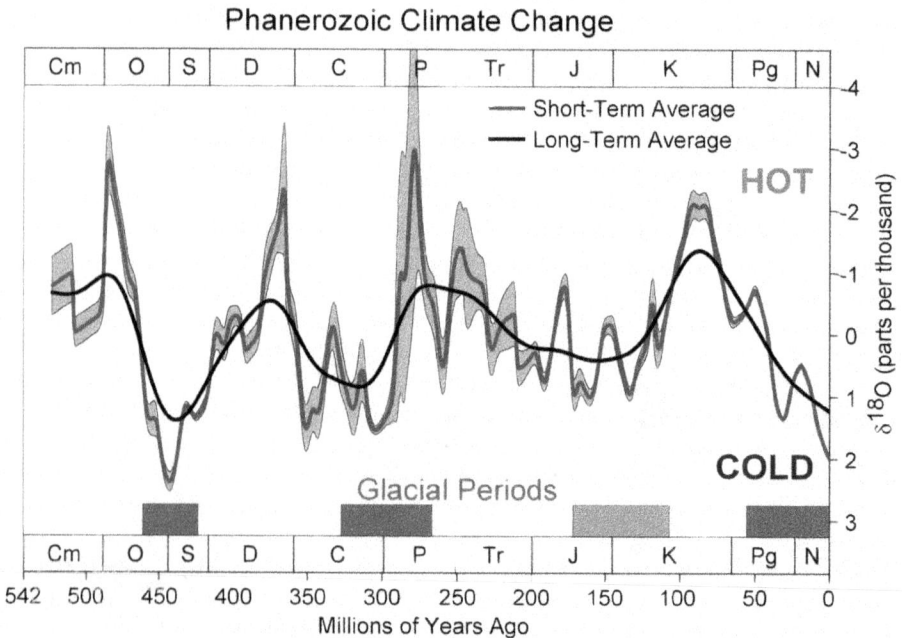

Figure 1.1. A 550-million-year record of ocean temperatures based on $^{18}O/^{16}O$ ratios from the shells of marine organisms. Data is from Vetzer et al., 1999.[7] Figure source: GNU Free Documentation License Version 1.2, November 2002 Copyright (©) 2000, 2001, 2002 Free Software Foundation, Inc.

^{18}O and ^{16}O are two stable isotopes of oxygen, and their ratios reflect the water temperature from which the shell material of marine organisms (calcium carbonate) was formed.[7] That is partly because ^{16}O is lighter than ^{18}O, so it evaporates faster from the oceans. But also, when global temperatures are relatively cool, ice caps develop at the earth's poles. As water vapor containing ^{18}O rains preferentially at lower latitudes it leaves more ^{16}O in the air. When that ^{16}O-rich air reaches the poles, it falls as snow. Snowfall, which feeds glacial ice, locks the ^{16}O in glaciers, further enriching ocean water in ^{18}O. This process is why carbonate shell material precipitated during cold global temperatures has a more positive δ^{18}O signature, reflecting the presence of more- "heavy" ^{18}O in the oceans. Conversely, when global temperatures are warmer, the δ^{18}O of carbonate shell material becomes more negative, reflecting more "light" in the oceans. The isotopic composition of carbonate shell material is how we know that the climate has repeatedly oscillated between warming and cooling trends throughout the history of the earth.

The reasons for this climatic variability, which are understood generally but certainly not completely, are the complex interactions between hundreds of factors that influence the earth's climate. Some of the factors that scientists generally agree affect the Earth's climate are shown in Figure 1.2. These factors can be placed into (at least) five different categories based on their origin. These categories include solar, orbital, tectonic, oceanic, and atmospheric factors.

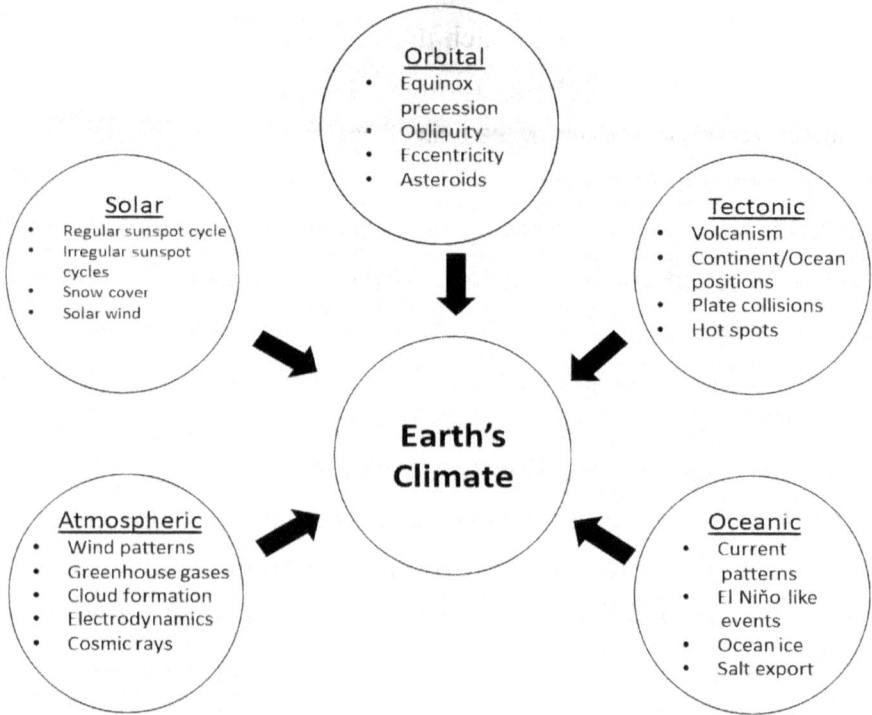

Figure 1.2. Major categories of factors that affect the Earth's climate.

The first category is solar factors. It's no particular secret that the earth's weather and climate is most directly affected by solar radiation, but the sun's radiation output is not constant over time. The most obvious change in solar radiation, one that is readily observable within the timeframe of a human lifetime, is the eleven-year sunspot cycle. Sunspots are caused by solar flares that increase overall radiation output by the sun. Thus, years characterized by many sunspots deliver more Total Solar Irradiation (TSI) to the earth than years with fewer or no sunspots.[8] But the sunspot cycle is not always constant. Between 1645 and 1700 CE, for example, a time known as the Maunder Minimum, sunspot activity was unusually low.[8] As one might expect, the amount of TSI reaching the earth decreased during the Maunder Minimum, contributing to the marked cooling trend of the Little Ice Age dur-ing that same time period. Furthermore, variations in snow and ice (both of which reflect incoming solar radiation back out into space) can reduce the amount of TSI reaching the earth. Finally, variations in the solar wind and cosmic rays reaching the earth can affect the atmosphere's electrodynamics, which regulates cloud formation and surface temperatures.[9]

The second category are orbital factors. The first, called the "pre-cession of the equinoxes," is caused by a slight wobble in the earth's spin axis. This wobble changes the timing of the two equinoxes and the summer and winter solstices. That, in turn, affects global temperatures in a cycle that lasts about 20,000 years. The second orbital factor, known as "obliquity," is governed by the tilt of the earth's spin axis. Pres-ently, the earth's spin axis is tilted at an angle of 23.5 degrees from the earth's orbital plane. That angle, however, changes over time between 22.1 and 24.5 degrees and accentuates or moderates the severity of seasonal temperature changes. The greater the Earth's axial tilt angle, the greater the temperature difference between summer and winter. It takes 41,000 years to complete one obliquity cycle. The eccentricity of the earth's orbit around the sun also changes over time. At present, the earth's orbit is near its most circular, and the earth is receiving more solar radiation than when the orbit is more elliptical. When the orbit becomes more elliptical, the earth receives less solar radiation. There are several components of orbital eccentricity that loosely combine to form a 100,000-year cycle. Finally, the earth's orbit inevitably brings it into contact with asteroids that are also orbiting the sun. About every 500,000 years or so, an asteroid with a diameter of a kilometer or more collides with the earth. Such collisions spew dust, ash, and aerosols into the atmosphere, which can block significant amounts of solar radiation from reaching the earth for long periods of time.

The third category, tectonic factors, are caused by the earth's heat dynamics. The earth's core is made predominantly of iron and nickel that, because of high density, naturally migrated to the center of the early earth when it was still fully molten. But because radioactive elements such as uranium are "siderophiles" (soluble in molten iron), they too migrated to the earth's core. The radioactive decay of those elements creates heat that must somehow disperse. The ocean-ridge volcanos that circle the earth are one way that heat is dispersed. Those ocean ridges, in turn, are separated by rigid plates on the earth's surface that are then pushed slowly by heat-driven convection currents in the earth's mantle. Those processes, known collectively as plate tectonics, drive the volcanic activity that causes periodic catastrophic volcanic explosions such as the Samalas eruption in 1257 CE. Also, plumes of molten rock produced near the earth's core can rise to the earth's surface as "hot spots" in places like Hawaii and Yellowstone Park, dispersing radiogenic heat by volcanic activity.

An important feature of the solar, orbital, and tectonic factors is that they are *entirely independent of each other*. How those factors line up with each other determines whether the earth's climate is warming or cooling at any given time. Those interactions, however, are constantly changing precisely because they are independent of each other. The Samalas eruption had enormous consequences for human populations in 1258 CE. But imagine what might have happened if the Samalas eruption had occurred during the Maunder Minimum? The cooling would have been even more dramatic. Suppose we had a situation in which obliquity and precession were maximized while the earth's orbit is at its most circular. The earth's climate would probably be much warmer than it is today, as it was in the Cambrian Period 550 million years ago, or in the Cretaceous Period 100 million years ago (Fig. 1.1).

Finally, the heat generated by the combined solar, orbital, and tectonic processes are dispersed unevenly around the planet by ocean currents and wind circulation patterns. In addition, the rate that heat is radiated from earth back to outer space is mediated by the concentrations of greenhouse gases present in the atmosphere, especially water vapor, carbon dioxide, and methane. The differing atmospheric temperatures around the planet also affect cloud formation, as do the solar wind and cosmic radiation. Clouds can be a major factor in how much solar radiation is reflected into space.

Consider how the earth's energy budget works averaged over a one-year period.[10] Based on satellite measurements, a yearly average flux of 342 Watts per meter squared (W/m^2) or equivalently 342 joules per second (J/sec), of solar energy reaches the earth's upper atmosphere (the left side of Fig. 1.3). Of that total, which consists largely of short-wave (0.2-2 micron (μm)) ultraviolet and visible radiation, 107 W/m^2 is immediately reflected into space either by clouds or by the earth's surface. The atmosphere absorbs 67 W/m^2 of energy, and the earth's surface absorbs an additional 168 W/m^2, producing long-wave (1.0 - 70 μm) infrared radiation (heat) of which 24 W/m^2 is distributed through the atmosphere by wind currents. Meanwhile (on the right side of Fig. 1.2), 390 W/m^2 of the long-wave thermal radiation is emitted into the atmosphere. Importantly, 324 W/m^2 of that long-wave radiation is intercepted by greenhouse gases, principally water vapor and carbon dioxide, and is back-radiated to the earth. This is the famous greenhouse effect, the principal process keeping the mean annual temperature of the earth's atmosphere above freezing. The remainder of the long-wave radiation (235 W/m^2) ultimately escapes back into outer space.

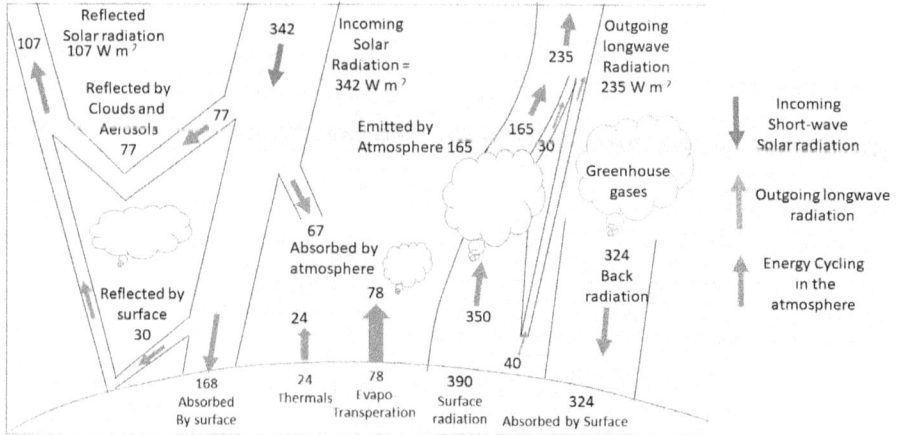

Figure 1.3 A conceptual model of the earth's mean annual energy budget. Data is from Kiehl and Trenberth, 1997. [10]

This energy budget balances over one year, with 342 W/m² being delivered to and then leaving the earth. It is evident that even small changes will alternately produce a net warming or cooling of the atmosphere. Most obviously, these changes are why days are warmer than nights and summers are warmer than winters. But at the same time, imbalances in how much energy enters and leaves the atmosphere over a variety of time frames determines whether there is an overall warming or cooling trend in earth's climate.

Given this delicate energy balance, it's no wonder that the earth's climate is always changing (Fig. 1.1). Because of the vast number of factors (Fig. 1.2) that can affect the atmosphere's energy balance (Fig. 1.3), and given that those factors are constantly changing and interacting with each other over time, climate stasis is virtually impossible.

Climate reversals, in other words, are inevitable.

⇔

There have been countless climate reversals during the five million years that humans and proto-humans have inhabited the earth. Therefore, it's reasonable to wonder how climate reversals, some of which have occurred gradually and some of which happened almost instantly, have affected human history. Did climate change contribute to the evolution of humanity in the first place? How did periodic catastrophic cooling events, such as those initiated by the Samalas volcanic explosion, affect human societies? Conversely, how did periodic warming events affect those societies as well? Could it be that the great migrations of people that occurred at the end of the Bronze Age (~1200 BCE) and at the end of the Roman Warm Period (~400 CE) have been caused, or at least influenced, by climate reversals?

The purpose of this book is to consider those kinds of questions. We can begin at the very dawn of earth's history four and a half billion years ago.

REFERENCES

1. Lavigne, F., Degeai, J.P., Komorowski, J.C., Guillet, S., Robert, V., Lahitte, P., Oppenheimer, C., Stoffel, M., Vidal, C.M., Pratomo, I. and Wassmer, P., 2013. Source of the great AD 1257 mystery eruption unveiled, Samalas volcano, Rinjani Volcanic Complex, Indonesia. Proceedings of the National Academy of Sciences, 110(42), pp.16742-16747.

2. Stothers, R.B., 2000. Climatic and demographic consequences of the massive volcanic eruption of 1258. Climatic Change, 45(2), pp.361-374.

3. Campbell, B.M., 2017. Global climates, the 1257 mega-eruption of Samalas volcano, Indonesia, and the English food crisis of 1258. Transactions of the Royal Historical Society, 27, pp.87-121.

4. Farris, W.W., 2006. Japan's Medieval Population: Famine, Fertility, and Warfare in a Transformative Age. University of Hawaii Press.

5. Guillet, S., Corona, C., Stoffel, M., Khodri, M., Lavigne, F., Ortega, P., Eckert, N., Sielenou, P.D., Daux, V., Churakova, O.V. and Davi, N., 2017. Climate response to the Samalas volcanic eruption in 1257

revealed by proxy records. Nature geoscience, 10(2), pp.123-128.

6. J.C. Russell, 1972. Population in Europe. In Carlo M. Cipolla, ed., The Fontana Economic History of Europe, Vol. I: The Middle Ages. Glasgow. Collins/Fontana, pp 25-71.

7. 2. Veizer, J., Ala, D., Azmy, K., Bruckschen, P., Buhl, D., Bruhn, F., Carden, G.A.F., Diener, A., Ebneth, S., Godderis, Y., Jasper, T., Korte, C., Pawellek, F., Podlaha, O. and Strauss, H. 1999. $^{87}Sr/^{86}Sr$, $\delta^{13}C$ and $\delta^{18}O$ evolution of Phanerozoic seawater. Chemical Geology 161, 59-88.

8. Kopp, G., Krivova, N., Wu, C.J. and Lean, J., 2016. The impact of the revised sunspot record on solar irradiance reconstructions. Solar Physics, 291(9), pp.2951-2965.

9. Cliver, E.W., Boriakoff, V. and Feynman, J., 1998. Solar variability and climate change: Geomagnetic aa index and global surface temperature. Geophysical Research Letters, 25(7), pp.1035-1038.

10. Kiehl, J.T. and Trenberth, K.E., 1997. Earth's annual global mean energy budget. Bulletin of the American meteorological society, 78(2), pp.197-208.

CHAPTER 2
Four Billion Years of Climate Change

THE CURRENTLY ACCEPTED AGE of the earth is 4.543 billion years old. For the first half billion years, there was little climate change because the earth didn't have an atmosphere and therefore had no climate. More accurately, the earth didn't have a *permanent* atmosphere. The earth was originally formed by gravity that attracted swarms of asteroids and meteorites circling the newly formed sun and accreting them into a single planet. The sun kept the bulk of the hydrogen leftover from a star that exploded long ago, whereas Venus, Earth, and Mars kept the bulk of the heavier elements such as silicon, oxygen, carbon, iron, and uranium. Those heavier elements, in turn, had been formed when the exploding star, probably a red giant, collapsed in on itself prior to exploding as a supernova. The early earth's atmosphere, principally hydrogen and helium, probably didn't last long. The explosions caused by the continuing bombardment of meteorites and asteroids would have swept most of the gases out into space. Also, because the earth didn't yet have a magnetic field, the sun's solar wind swept away whatever gases the asteroids left behind.

The thermal energy created by the asteroid bombardment, working in concert with the decay of radioactive elements like uranium, soon (in a few million years) turned the early earth into a ball of hot molten magma. The heaviest elements (the iron, nickel and much of the uranium) sank down to the middle of the planet and formed the earth's core. The lighter elements, silica and oxygen, floated to the surface and crystallized, forming what eventually became the earth's crust. Much of the oxygen combined with hydrogen to form water vapor, initiating a permanent atmosphere and ushering in some semblance of a climate.

The first atmosphere was probably composed mostly of steam with a mix of carbon dioxide, hydrogen sulfide, and methane. The molten iron-nickel core of the new earth, combined with the planet's rotation, created a magnetic field that deflected the solar wind, allowing the new atmosphere to accumulate. Mars, incidentally, doesn't have a magnetic field, which is one reason most of its water was swept out into space long ago. By the time the earth was half a billion years old, the steam in the atmosphere cooled and liquefied into water, creating what would become oceans. That's the extent of what we can glean about the earth's climate in the beginning. The temperature was cool enough for liquid water to form and warm enough for water vapor to coexist with liquid water.

The result of a miraculous confluence of the earth's distance from the sun, the earth's newly developed magnetic field, and the presence of greenhouse gases (water vapor, carbon dioxide, and methane) in the atmosphere, that temperature range meant that life could develop. And, by 3.5 billion years ago, life had indeed appeared. For the first billion years, this life consisted of single-celled archaea that inhabited hot springs discharging into the oceans. By 2.46 billion years ago, however, some microorganisms developed the ability to extract energy from sunlight by means of photosynthesis. The overall process of photosynthesis consumes carbon dioxide and water and produces sugar (glucose) and molecular oxygen (O_2):

$$6CO_2 \quad + \quad 6H_2O \quad + \quad light \quad \rightarrow \quad C_6H_{12}O_6 \quad + \quad 6O_2 \qquad \text{Equation 2.1}$$

Carbon   water   glucose   oxygen

dioxide   (gas)

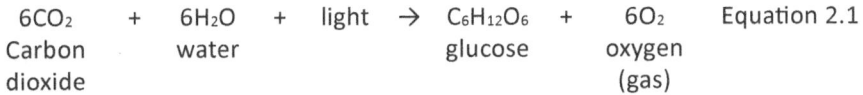

In the space of just a few million years, the gaseous oxygen released by photosynthesis accumulated in the atmosphere, completely changing how life on earth would eventually develop. The Great Oxidation Event as it is called (the process of changing the earth's atmosphere from its former oxygen-free condition to being oxygenated) also contributed to earth's first climate reversal. Specifically, most of the earth froze.[1]

For a billion years or so prior, the earth's climate had largely maintained a temperature range that allowed both liquid water in the oceans and water vapor in the atmosphere to coexist. One reason for this more consistent temperature range was the presence of greenhouse gases that trapped the sun's radiation as heat (Fig. 1.3), effectively buffering the atmosphere's temperature between about 10°C and 80°C. The introduction of oxygen, however, upset the delicate balance of the three most important atmospheric greenhouse gases: water vapor, carbon dioxide, and methane. Carbon dioxide, the basic substrate of photosynthesis (Equation 1), was systematically removed from the atmosphere and turned into cellular organic carbon. Methane, a much more powerful greenhouse gas than carbon dioxide, is chemically unstable in the presence of oxygen and sunlight, and so methane concentrations decreased as well. With lower concentrations of carbon dioxide and methane, the atmosphere cooled, reducing the amount of water vapor (also a greenhouse gas) the air could hold. With less temperature-buffering provided by greenhouse gases, snow accumulated on land masses and reflected more shortwave radiation into space. Eventually, the entire earth froze 2.46 billion years ago, creating what geologists call a "snowball" earth.

This was the first, and arguably the most dramatic, climate reversal in earth history.

The earth seems to have frozen and thawed at least three times between 2.46 and 2.25 billion years ago[2], an interval of 200 million years. The geologic evidence for this very long, very cold, and very bizarre period of earth's history can be found on at least four present-day continents: North America, Eurasia, Southern Africa, and Australia. At the time of the first snowball earth episode, a large landmass approaching the size of a supercontinent was located astride the equator and was covered by glaciers. Because of their vast ability to grind up rocks and carry them long distances, glaciers produce very distinctive sedimentary deposits. In North America, for example, sedimentary rocks from the Huronian Supergroup of Canada, which were deposited during or just after one of these "snowball" events, contain what geologists call "dropstones." When a glacier grinds up rocks, some of the rock fragments are picked up by the ice and transported in whatever direction the glacier is moving. In what is now Canada, the glaciers ground up the ancient red granites of the Canadian Shield and transported them toward the surrounding ocean. As the glaciers broke up and formed icebergs, they floated out to sea and gradually melted, releasing ground-up fragments of red granite that sunk and were incorporated into the fine-grained clays covering the ocean floor. The black shale that those fine-grained sediments eventually became, therefore, also contains chunks of broken-up red granite. Today, rocks containing dropstones have eroded out of the Huronian Supergroup and can be found on the shores of Lake Huron (Figure 2.1), transported by glaciers during our last ice age 20,000 years ago. The fact that this is a black shale is also significant. During these glacial intervals the production, deposition, and burial of organic carbon was accelerating.[2] The organic carbon in this rock (Fig. 2.1) is what makes it a "black" shale.

Figure 2.1. Chunks of red granite embedded in a sedimentary rock from the Huronian Supergroup. The granite fragments had been ground up by glaciers on the Canadian Shield 2.25 billion years ago, transported to the surrounding ocean, rafted out to sea by icebergs, and finally dropped to the seafloor forming a black shale. [Pocket knife is for scale.]

The geologic evidence that the snowball earth glaciations were related in some way to the Great Oxidation Event (GOE) is intriguing and hinges on the four stable isotopes of sulfur: ^{32}S, ^{33}S, ^{34}S, ^{36}S. Because of their differing atomic masses, these isotopes behave slightly differently when undergoing chemical or biological reactions. Most natural processes, such as the reaction of atmospheric sulfur dioxide (SO_2) with oxygen (O_2), fractionate sulfur isotopes in proportion to their differing masses. That kind of process is called a "mass-dependent" fractionation. Other chemical processes, such as ultraviolet photolysis of atmospheric sulfur dioxide, produce a "mass-independent" fractionation.[3]

Volcanos have been delivering sulfur compounds such as sulfur dioxide and hydrogen sulfide to the atmosphere for most of earth's history. But sulfur minerals formed in sediments deposited prior to the GOE do not exhibit mass-dependent fraction. That could only happen if there were not significant amounts of molecular oxygen in the atmosphere. Conversely, between 2.50 and 2.43 billion years ago, sulfur minerals exhibited significant mass-dependent fractionation, indicating the presence of oxygen in the atmosphere, effectively dating the GOE.[4]

Did the GOE cause the snowball earth glaciation event by stripping out greenhouse gases, or were there other processes at work? The geologic evidence suggests that several other factors may have contributed to the colder temperatures. Prior to the GOE, as that aforementioned large landmass began breaking apart, new tectonic spreading centers resulted in a massive outpouring of basaltic lava that spread over the fragments of the supercontinent. That formed a series of Large Igneous Provinces, or LIPs. Rocks of basaltic LIPs contain large amounts of iron and are unusual among igneous rocks for their relatively high phosphorous content. As those basaltic rocks weathered, large amounts of phosphorous and iron were delivered to the surrounding seas, acting as a fertilizer for the microorganisms living in those seas (particularly near the equator) and accelerating the production of cellular organic carbon. Because most of that carbon had to derive from carbon dioxide, concentrations of carbon dioxide in the atmosphere would have decreased dramatically, contributing to cooling. As snow and ice accumulated on the land masses, more and more solar energy was reflected into space, accelerating the cooling. Therefore, it probably wasn't solely the GOE that triggered the snowball earth. It was also the presence of a supercontinent located near the equator, the breakup of that supercontinent causing extensive volcanic activity, and the weathering of those basalts that further stimulated microbial sequestration of carbon dioxide. These multiple triggers illustrate an important generality about climate change: It almost always reflects a combination of processes and/or events rather than a single distinct cause.

One reason we think that some combination of those tectonic, chemical, and biological processes caused the first Paleoproterozoic snowball earth episodes is that more than a billion years later, something similar happened that produced another series of snowball earth events. Those events, known as the Neoproterozoic Snowball Earth, seem to have been triggered by an eerily similar sequence of events. Once again, a supercontinent named Rodinia had assembled itself somewhere near the equator. Once again, that supercontinent broke up with the emplacement of basaltic LIPs on the continental fragments. As those iron and phosphorous-rich rocks weathered, the surrounding seas were "fertilized," there was a bloom of microorganisms, carbon dioxide was stripped from the atmosphere, and three snowball-earth episodes were the result between 700 million and 620 million years ago.[5]

More importantly for life on earth, those same processes later produced a second Great Oxidation Event (GOE-2) about 620 million years ago. In this case, a continental collision between East and West Gondwana produced an 8,000-mile-long mountain chain known as the Transgondwanan Supermountains. Once again, as these mountains eroded, iron and phosphorous nutrients were delivered to the surrounding seas, triggering an explosion of oxygen-producing algae and cyanobacteria populations.[6] After GOE-1, the atmosphere was oxygenated, but at fairly low O_2 concentrations of probably less than 5%. After GOE-2, however, O_2 increased to about 20%. Those O_2 concentrations permitted multicellular organisms to thrive, leading to the Great Cambrian Explosion of multi-cellular life 530 million years ago.

While we've seen a variety of events and processes that might have caused the snowball earth events, the next question is what happened to end snowball earth events? During a snowball earth deep freeze, biological consumption of carbon dioxide was severely constrained whereas carbon dioxide production from volcanos around the world continued unabated, causing carbon dioxide concentrations in the atmosphere to gradually rise, eventually reaching levels high enough to warm the atmosphere again. As ice melted, the albedo effect was lessened, causing more warming. As the climate warmed, the atmosphere could hold more water vapor, also a powerful greenhouse gas, further accelerating the warming process. As the oceans warmed, carbon dioxide dissolved in ocean water disassociated into carbonate, combined with dissolved calcium, and precipitated as calcium carbonate. These "carbonate capstones" at the top of a sequence of glacial sediments record the final warming phase after a snowball earth event.[7]

The last snowball earth event, known as the Gaskiers Glaciation, ended 620 million years ago, and the carbon dioxide-charged atmosphere warmed the oceans to much higher temperatures than they are today. By the Cambrian Period (541 MY), the beginning of the Phanerozoic Eon, ocean temperatures were as high as 60° C (Figure 2.1).[8] Because of the fossil shells that appeared in the Phanerozoic (literally "visible life"), and because the oxygen isotopes contained in that shell material give an indication of ocean temperature, the temperature record is much more detailed than the record of the Paleoproterozoic or Neoproterozoic snowball earth events. Interestingly, that record (Fig. 1.1) suggests that the Phanerozoic Eon has been a time of steadily cooling temperatures following the high post-Gaskiers Glaciation temperatures.

The larger point, once again, is that the earth's temperature has never been stationary for any length of time, and it varies between extreme cold (snowball earth events) to the very warm seas that dominated the earth during the early Paleozoic Period. In more recent times, certainly since fully modern humans appeared 100,000 years ago, these temperature variations have been particularly violent, and they seem to have played a significant role in how humans evolved in the first place.

That is the topic we will look at next.

REFERENCES

1. Hoffman, P.F., 2013. The Great Oxidation and a Siderian snowball Earth: MIF-S based correlation of Paleoproterozoic glacial epochs. Chemical Geology, 362, pp.143-156.

2. Gumsley, A.P., Chamberlain, K.R., Bleeker, W., Söderlund, U., de Kock, M.O., Larsson, E.R. and Bekker, A., 2017. Timing and tempo of the GOE. Proceedings of the National Academy of Sciences, 114(8), pp.1811-1816.

3. Halevy, I., Johnston, D.T. and Schrag, D.P., 2010. Explaining the structure of the Archean mass-independent sulfur isotope record. Science, 329(5988), pp.204-207.

4. Warke, M.R., Di Rocco, T., Zerkle, A.L., Lepland, A., Prave, A.R., Martin, A.P., Ueno, Y., Condon, D.J. and Claire, M.W., 2020. The GOE preceded a paleoproterozoic "snowball Earth". Proceedings of the National Academy of Sciences, 117(24), pp.13314-13320.

5. Cox, G.M., Halverson, G.P., Stevenson, R.K., Vokaty, M., Poirier, A., Kunzmann, M., Li, Z.X., Denyszyn, S.W., Strauss, J.V. and Macdonald, F.A., 2016. Continental flood basalt weathering as a trigger for Neoproterozoic Snowball Earth. Earth and Planetary Science Letters, 446, pp.89-99.

6. Campbell, I.H. and Squire, R.J., 2010. The mountains that triggered the Late Neoproterozoic increase in oxygen: the Second Great Oxidation Event. Geochimica et Cosmochimica Acta, 74(15), pp.4187-4206.

7. Hoffmann, P.F. and Schrag, D.P., 2000. Snowball earth. Scientific American, 282(1), pp.68-75.

8. Veizer, J. and Prokoph, A., 2015. Temperatures and oxygen isotopic composition of Phanerozoic oceans. Earth-Science Reviews, 146, pp.92-104.

CHAPTER 3

Climate Change and the Origins of Humanity

HOW DID HUMANS BECOME HUMAN? That question has fascinated people since time immemorial. Every culture on earth has its own "creation story," a narrative of how and why people came to be. For example, the Mayans of South America told the following story:

> *In the beginning, Tepeu the maker and Gucumatz the feathered spirit used their powers to create the world. They created animals to look after the world and man to look after the animals. First, they tried to make man out of clay, but they found he crumbled into dust. Next, they tried to make man out of wood, but found he had an empty head and an empty heart. In the end, they made man out of corn, which satisfied the spirits because he had understanding and could care for the animals.*

It's only natural for people to want to know how and why they had come to be, and that's why there are so many creation stories around the world. The real origins of humanity, which have been worked out over the last century and a half by anthropologists, is almost as improbable as the Mayan story given above.

Because those origins seem to have been driven by climate change.

⇔

Louis Leakey (1903-1972) was the son of Christian missionaries to the Kikuyu tribe of Kenya and Louis was born near the present city of Nairobi. Raised among the Kikuyu, Louis learned their language and for a time lived in a Kikuyu-styled hut when he was a boy. Louis' father, Harry Leakey, was interested in natural science and co-founded the East Africa and Uganda Natural History Society. It was through that association that Louis met Arthur Loveridge, the first curator (1914) of the Natural History Museum in Nairobi, who encouraged Louis' interest in archaeology and anthropology.

Louis entered Cambridge University in 1922 intending to become a missionary like his parents. In 1924, however, Louis learned that the British Museum of Natural History was planning an expedition to the ex-German colony of Tanganyika to hunt for dinosaur fossils that had been discovered before World War I. Louis applied to join the expedition, was accepted, and was tasked with managing the logistics of the expedition as well as helping to find the fossil sites. After this mostly unsuccessful expedition, Louis returned to Cambridge to complete his studies, but the experience of fossil hunting led him to shift his studies to the natural sciences. In 1926 he graduated with honors in anthropology and archaeology. More importantly, Cambridge was impressed enough with his performance that they sent him back to Africa to study prehistoric sites that had once possibly been occupied by humans.

Also in 1924, an Australian anatomist named Raymond Dart working in South Africa was sent two crates of fossils recovered from a limestone mine near the small town of Taung. A small skull imbedded in the limestone resembled that of an ape. But anatomist Dart immediately recognized that, because of the location of the foramen magnum (the opening at the base of a skull where the spinal cord attaches to the brain), this creature had walked upright on two legs rather than shuffling about on all fours like apes. Dart's discovery, along with Louis' own excavations that unearthed stone tools clearly made by humans, convinced Leakey that Africa, not Europe (as most anthropologists thought in the 1920s), was where humans had first evolved. Resolving to find further evidence of his hypothesis, Leakey returned to Cambridge for graduate studies and received his Ph.D. in 1930 when he was twenty-seven years old.

Some years earlier in 1913, a German paleontologist named Hans Reck had excavated a site in Tanganyika on the eastern side of the Serengeti Plain known as Olduvai Gorge. That excavation yielded what seemed to be a human skeleton. World War I interrupted Reck's work, and after the war Germany ceded Tanganyika to Britain, effectively barring Reck from returning. With his new Ph.D. in hand, Leakey organized an expedition to Olduvai and invited Reck. The expedition uncovered fossils of various animals but more importantly they also found large numbers of stone tools, a clear indication of human or pre-human occupation.

Upon returning to Cambridge, however, Leakey's findings were met with skepticism. The anthropological thinking at that time, heavily influenced by the Piltdown Man hoax perpetrated in 1912, was that humans first appeared in Europe. Nonetheless, Louis continued to lecture on his findings, expressing his contention that Africa was the place to look for pre-human fossils. After one such lecture, Louis was introduced to a young archaeological illustrator named Mary Nicol. After a collaboration, in which Mary prepared the illustrations for Louis' book *Adam's Ancestors* (1934), the relationship turned romantic and the couple married in 1936.

The marriage of Louis and Mary Leakey would turn out to be pivotal for paleoanthropology. In Mary, Louis found a true soulmate, as dedicated as he was to searching for the precursors of modern humans. In Louis, Mary found someone willing and able to move heaven and earth to find the resources necessary to pursue that goal. The Leakeys returned to Kenya in 1937 where World War II eventually delayed their plans for searching for fossil hominins (as pre-humans are now called). During the war, Louis worked with British counterintelligence, recruiting a clandestine network of informers from among his boyhood Kikuyu friends. Mary took a job with the Coryndon Memorial Museum (later called the National Museums of Kenya), enabling her to continue excavations when time was available. Their first son, Jonathon, was born in 1940 and their second son, Richard, was born in 1944. With the end of the war, Louis became Curator of the Coryndon Museum with the express intention of resuming his and Mary's research in paleoanthropology.

Beginning in 1951, Louis and Mary began what were to become a series of extensive excavations at Olduvai Gorge. Those excavations recovered many non-human fossils and a great abundance of stone tools, which Mary lovingly illustrated. It wasn't until 1959, however, that Mary discovered the skull of a hominin that she always subsequently referred to as "Dear Boy." They later formally named the creature *Zinjanthropus*, but it now bears the name of *Paranthropus boisei*. Mary's pivotal find drew the attention of the National Geographic Society who provided funding for the Olduvai excavation, and who continued to support the Leakey family research for decades afterward.

Over the next half century, first Louis and Mary and then their second son Richard discovered numerous hominin fossils that have contributed mightily to our understanding of human origins. After Richard retired from paleoanthropology to enter Kenyan politics and his wife Meave Leakey took over leading the annual field expeditions, they began to understand how climate change had affected the ecology and evolution of life in East Africa.

By the 1970s, the Leakeys and numerous other paleoanthropologists working in Africa had clearly demonstrated that hominins were fully bipedal (walking upright on two legs) by three and a half million years ago. The rub was that DNA evidence suggested that the common ancestors of the hominin and chimpanzee lines had diverged about 5.5 million years ago. What happened during those intervening two million years? Meave Leakey resolved to see if she could find evidence of hominin evolutionary progress during that time period and hoped to find fossils dating to the time of the chimpanzee-hominin divergence.

Beginning in 1989, Meave systematically explored a site near Lake Turkana in Kenya that the native population called Lothagam Hill, a reference to its rough and varied landscape. The "hill" is a geologic horst, a block of rock that has remained uplifted in place while the landscape on either side of it was downfaulted. It effectively exposed sediments and sedimentary rocks ranging from fourteen to four million years old, precisely the time period Meave wanted to investigate. The older sediments of fourteen to nine million years old contained mostly fossilized wood, reflecting the tropical forests that covered much of the landscape during that time. Those tropical forests were home to a wide variety of monkeys and apes.[1] But, beginning about nine million years ago, the climate and the landscape began to change.

The sediments and sedimentary rocks at Lothagam consisted of mudstones, sandstones, and conglomerates deposited by what must have been an impressive river-lake system.[2] Many of these sediments show the distinctive "fining upward" sequence characteristic of meandering rivers. The base of each sequence consists of coarse-grained conglomerates that fine upward into sandstones, which then fine upward to mudstones. The coarse-grained conglomerates reflect the fast-moving water in the center of a river channel. As the channel migrates laterally, however, the water velocity decreases, leading to the deposition of finer-grained sands. At the top of the sequence, if it survives erosion by subsequent channel migrations, are mudstones characteristic of a broad flood plain.

The fossils preserved in the Lothagam sediments reflect the sorts of creatures one would expect to find in African rivers and lakes. The most common fossils were hippos, crocodiles, turtles, fish, and aquatic birds of all sorts. Importantly, but very rarely, fossil hominins were also found. But the real story of the Lothagam fossil assemblage is that it reflects a dramatic shift in the climate of that part of Africa: the climate became warmer and drier. By five to six million years ago, the thick tropical jungles recorded by the fossil wood found in the older Lothagam sediments were gone, having been replaced by grassland savannahs. Such a major shift in vegetation caused an equally major change in the kinds of herbivores that could exploit this new landscape.

The most telling change was the extinction of many species that had dominated the Lothagam landscape from nine to five million years ago.[3] Several species of old-world monkeys, including some tree-dwelling columbines, dropped out of the fossil record. Those extinctions would be expected if the tropical jungles largely ceased to exist. In addition, several species of horses came to an end at the same time, replaced by at least two new species of horses. That, too, would be expected if horses initially adapted to jungle life were forced to live on grassy plains. Several species of large antelopes exited the fossil record to be replaced by smaller, lighter antelopes and gazelles. Finally, the shift from larger to smaller antelopes probably also led to the extinction of some large predators, in particular the saber-toothed tiger.

Besides the extinctions that occurred around five million years ago, the more compelling evidence for a changing, warming climate comes from the carbon isotopic composition of fossil teeth. In humid, wet climates characteristic of jungle ecosystems, plants are dominated by C-3 plants called that because they produce a three-carbon compound (3-phosphoglycerate) during photosynthesis. C-3 plants are the most common kinds of plants on earth because they thrive in relatively cool, humid conditions. Under hot, dry conditions, however, C-3 plants close their stomata (pores that draw CO_2 into the plant) to reduce water loss. That might save water, but without CO_2, the plant can't proceed with photosynthesis. C-4 plants solve that problem by adding an additional step in their photosynthesis that produces a four-carbon compound (oxaloacetic acid) that allows carbon fixation while their stomata remain closed, thus saving water. In other words, in places that are hot, dry, and generally water-starved—places like east Africa today—C-4 plants have a serious competitive advantage over C-3 plants.

So how can we determine if herbivores were eating C-3 or C-4 plants five million years ago? The answer is in their teeth. Carbon has two stable isotopes: ^{12}C and ^{13}C. Because of the different ways C-3 and C-4 plants grab the CO_2 for photosynthesis, they differ in how much ^{12}C and ^{13}C they extract from carbon dioxide in the air. Specifically, C-4 plants absorb more ^{13}C carbon than C-3 plants. The ^{13}C to ^{12}C ratio preserved in herbivore teeth, therefore, records the relative portion of C-3 to C-4 plants in their diet. C-3 plants in a canopied jungle typically have a $\delta^{13}C$ (a standardized measure of the C-13/C-12 ratio) of about -27 per mil. A C-4 grass on an arid plain has a less negative $\delta^{13}C$ of about -13 per mil. An herbivore eating C-3 plants, as a result, develops tooth enamel with a $\delta^{13}C$ signature that is more negative than an herbivore eating C-4 plants. Prior to five million years ago, fossil teeth of antelopes recovered from Lothagam were eating C-3 jungle plants almost exclusively. After five million years ago, the antelopes were mostly eating C-4 plants.[4] Clearly, the extinctions around five million years ago were related to the changing climate and the changing plants on the landscape.

While all this was taking place, the hominins living in east Africa were also changing and adapting to this new grassy landscape. While most fossils found at Lothagam were of animals, a few hominin fossils were also found.[5] Furthermore, the oldest of these hominin fossils (two isolated teeth) are dated between five and six million years old. This date would place them at about the same time of the Lothagam animal extinctions and about the same time of the hominin-chimpanzee divergence 5.5 million years ago, just as Meave Leakey had hoped.

The Lothagam fossil assemblages provided solid evidence of climatic change and clearly indicates that between nine and five million years ago, the east African climate became hotter and drier. Interestingly, there is also evidence that the climate in other parts of the world—notably Pakistan and North America—experienced a change toward hotter and drier conditions during that time period.[6] So, can we conclude that the time period between nine and five million years ago was a time of global warming?

The answer, curiously enough, is no. About sixty million years ago, the world's oceans began a long cooling trend that accelerated ten million years ago (Fig. 1.1).

So, was the last ten million years a time of global warming or cooling? The answer seems to be that while it was a time of oceanic cooling, it was also a time of atmospheric warming in some parts of the world. The average temperature of seawater had been getting cooler for the last sixty million years. But beginning ten million years ago, the average atmospheric temperature of continental east Africa, North America, and East Asia became hotter and drier.[6] How can that possibly have been the case? This contrast only makes sense when one considers the complex interaction of atmospheric processes that affect global and regional climates.[7]

Several hypotheses have been advanced to explain the "Late Miocene global cooling" event, as the oceanic cooling is called. One possibility is that the relatively low atmospheric concentrations of CO_2 that prevailed at the time may have triggered cooling.[8] Other researchers have proposed that the interaction between astronomical processes, in particular the precession of the equinoxes and the obliquity of the earth's axis, may explain or at least contribute to the observed cooling.[9]

Atmospheric modelers, on the other hand, have suggested that as the Sahara Desert Africa became more arid, it may have increased the southward transport of atmospheric heat towards the equator[10], making east Africa hotter and drier. Another idea is that the initiation of glaciation in Antarctica ten million years ago may have caused an upwelling of cold water that cooled the oceans nearer the equator.[11] Finally, geologists have suggested that the cooling over the last sixty million years may be related to the tectonic opening of the Atlantic Ocean between Africa and the Americas. That opening, in turn, could facilitate ocean currents to transport cool water from the south polar oceans towards the equator.[12]

As is often the case, it's difficult to evaluate all of those hypotheses. There is, however, physical evidence that the wet-dry (cool-hot) cycles in East Africa are related to both equinox precession (wobbling) and the obliquity (tilt) of the earth's rotational axis. The hominin fossil-bearing sediments of the Lake Turkana region are highly cyclic in nature. That is to say the texture of the lacustrine sediments changes predictably with sandstones (lower lake level, drier climate) being overlain by claystones. That sandstone-claystone sequence then repeats itself over and over again in cycles that are visually very striking. Craig Feibel and his colleagues interpreted those repeating sequences as representing the rise and fall of water levels in Lake Turkana and the rivers feeding the lake over the last two million years. High water levels (claystones) imply a wetter climate, whereas the lower water levels (sandstones) imply a drier climate. Because the Turkana basin is volcanically active, periodic eruptions produce beds of volcanic ash that are interbedded with the lake sediments. Those ashes, which can be dated quite accurately, show how long it took each wet-dry cycle to form. When Feibel compared the dates associated with each sedimentary cycle, he found that each took about 20,000 years to form, suggesting that both the precession of the equinoxes (~20,000-year cycle) and obliquity (~40,000 year-cycle) may have been responsible for, or at least contributed to, the observed changes in climate.[13]

So how and why did hominins appear in the fossil record about five million years ago in Africa? We know that the common human/chimpanzee ancestor walked on all fours, spent considerable time in trees, and ate a diet consisting mostly of C-3 plants. It probably had fur like a modern chimpanzee and teeth adapted to a diet of leaves and fruit. Moving five million years to the present, we know that modern *Homo sapiens* are bipedal, spend most of their time on the ground, and eat a varied omnivorous diet consisting of plants, animals, and animal products and have an unusually large and complex brain. The fur, while still present in vestigial form, is barely visible in modern humans.

What, from an ecological point of view, could explain the development of those uniquely human traits? One interpretation is that the chimpanzees stayed in their forests, shrinking though they were, and continued with a forest lifestyle. Hominins, on the other hand, either chose or were forced onto the grassy savannahs where they faced a whole new set of ecological challenges. The best way for the new hominins to succeed on the savannah was to identify and exploit a new and separate ecological niche, one that became available because of the changing climate. The increasingly hot, dry climate caused many animal species to become largely nocturnal, thus avoiding the heat of the day. That change opened a niche for hominins to become predominantly diurnal, being active primarily during the day.

But accessing this new diurnal niche would require changes in how the emerging hominins moved about, how they dealt with the heat of the day, and how they foraged for food. Apes and chimpanzees move about on all fours, which is a relatively inefficient means of locomotion. Walking and running on two legs, in contrast, is extremely energy efficient. It's true that modern humans can't run as fast as four-footed creatures, at least in a sprint. But because of the energy efficiency inherent in bipedal locomotion, modern humans can outrun just about any quadrupedal animal, including horses and dogs, over long distances. That energy efficiency also enabled hominins to range long distances in the search for food. And because they could perspire to stay cool, they could forage during the heat of the day, thus avoiding nocturnal predators. Losing the fur and operating during the day also meant the skin would have to produce melanin to protect itself from damaging ultraviolet radiation.

Another opportunity that this diurnal niche offered was the changing food supply that became available on the open plains. Grasses and sedges, which are predominantly C-4 plants, make seeds and stems that can be a good source of both lipids and carbohydrates. Similarly, tubers, which grow underground on the plains, are also a potential source of carbohydrates. Other things like grasshoppers, termites, bird's eggs, crustaceans, and grubs can provide nutrition. Finally, scavenging meat and bone marrow from kills of other predators was another potential food source. Adopting an omnivorous diet opened up new sources of high-calorie food.

Becoming a dietary generalist had two important consequences. First and most importantly, a diet that included meat and animal fat provided a caloric boost enabling the hominin brain to become larger and more complex. The modern human brain comprises only about 2% of a person's overall body weight, but it consumes up to 20% of a person's caloric intake. Without access to a calorie-rich diet that included animal fat, there was no metabolic room for the hominin brain to become larger. Some hominins such as *Homo erectus* adopted the omnivore lifestyle and evolved progressively larger brains over time. Other hominins, such as *Paranthropus boisei*, ate plants exclusively and their brains did not increase in size at all over the 1.5 million years of their evolutionary life. Being a dietary generalist also meant that people could inhabit just about any environment on earth. Successive waves of hominins, beginning with *Homo erectus* about 1.5 million years ago and culminating with modern *Homo sapiens* 100,000 years ago, left Africa and spread out across the globe.

By 100,000 years ago, humans had developed a set of physical and mental traits atypical for mammals. These traits include bipedalism, almost exclusive diurnal activity, heat tolerance, and an omnivorous diet. One of the oddest, however, is the fact that human women undergo menopause in their later years and cease being able to bear children. That characteristic is almost unknown in other mammalian species whose females remain fertile for their entire adult lives. But not human women. Why would that be?

The answer seems to be something that has been termed the "grand-mother effect." One of the biological downsides of having a large and complicated brain is that it takes a long time to fully develop and train. As the hominin brain became larger over time, the length of childhood became progressively longer to allow the brain to develop and for the child to learn. This longer childhood puts an enormous strain on both human parents, but particularly on the women who spend a dispropor-tionate amount of time caring for young children. One biological way to address this problem is to extend the lifespan of women. With a longer lifespan, women can live to become grandmothers and actively care for their children's children. How is a woman's lifespan increased? An evolutionary biochemical mechanism—menopause—that actively shuts down fertility later in life. Menopause takes away the dangers inherent with pregnancy and childbirth, allows grandmothers to live longer, and enables them to assist in raising their grandchildren, increasing the survival rate of those grandchildren. It has been demonstrated with pre-modern demographic records that women with prolonged post-reproductive lifespans tend to have more surviving grandchildren, and therefore greater biological fitness, than those with shorter post-reproductive lives.[14]

⇔

The real-life creation story of how hominins evolved into humans may not be as poetic as *in the end, they made man out of corn, which satisfied the spirits because he had understanding and could care for the animals*, but it is interesting that climate change seems to have been a major factor driving that evolution. The environmental stresses imposed by a constantly changing climate are the principal reason that some established species sink into extinction and are replaced by new species. The global ocean cooling that began sixty million years ago and accelerated ten million years ago paradoxically resulted in regional warming of east and southern Africa.

If it had not been for climate change, humans may never have evolved the way they did.

REFERENCES

1. Harrison, T., 2016. Miocene primates. The International Encyclopedia of Primatology, pp.1-5.

2. Feibel, C.S., 2003. Stratigraphy and depositional history of the Lothagam sequence. Lothagam: The Dawn of Humanity in Eastern Africa. Columbia University Press, New York, pp.17-29.

3. Leakey, M.G. and Harris, J.M., 2003. Lothagam: its significance and contributions. Lothagam: The Dawn of Humanity in Eastern Africa. Columbia University Press, New York, pp.625-660.

4. Cerling, T.E., Harris, J.M., Leakey, M G and Mudida, N., 2003. Stable isotope ecology of northern Kenya, with emphasis on the Turkana Basin. In Lothagam: The Dawn of Humanity in Eastern Africa. Columbia University Press, New York, pp.583-603.

5. Leakey, M.G. and Walker, A.C., 2003. The Lothagam Hominids. In Lothagam: The Dawn of Humanity in Eastern Africa. Columbia University Press, New York, pp. 249-258.

6. Cerling, T.E., Harris, J.M., MacFadden, B.J., Leakey, M.G., Quade, J., Eisenmann, V. and Ehleringer, J.R., 1997. Global vegetation change through the Miocene/Pliocene boundary. Nature, 389(6647), pp.153-158.

7. Veizer, J. and Prokoph, A., 2015. Temperatures and oxygen isotopic composition of Phanerozoic oceans. Earth-Science Reviews, 146, pp.92-104.

8. Herbert, T.D., Lawrence, K.T., Tzanova, A., Peterson, L.C., Caballero-Gill, R. and Kelly, C.S., 2016. Late Miocene global cooling and the rise of modern ecosystems. Nature Geoscience, 9(11), pp.843-847.

9. Holbourn, A., Kuhnt, W., Clemens, S., Prell, W. and Andersen, N., 2013. Middle to late Miocene stepwise climate cooling: Evidence from a high-resolution deep water isotope curve spanning 8 million years. Paleoceanography, 28(4), pp.688-699.

10. Micheels, A., Eronen, J. and Mosbrugger, V., 2009. The Late Miocene climate response to a modern Sahara desert. Global and Planetary Change, 67(3-4), pp.193-204.

11. Heinrich, S., Zonneveld, K.A., Bickert, T. and Willems, H., 2011. The Benguela upwelling related to the Miocene cooling events and the development of the Antarctic circumpolar current: evidence from calcareous dinoflagellate cysts. Paleoceanography, 26(3).

12. Friedrich, O., Norris, R.D. and Erbacher, J., 2012. Evolution of middle to Late Cretaceous oceans—a 55 my record of Earth's temperature and carbon cycle. Geology, 40(2), pp.107-110.

13. Lepre, C.J., Quinn, R.L., Joordens, J.C., Swisher III, C.C. and Feibel,

C.S., 2007. Plio-Pleistocene facies environments from the KBS Member, Koobi Fora Formation: implications for climate controls on the development of lake-margin hominin habitats in the northeast Turkana Basin (northwest Kenya). Journal of Human Evolution, 53(5), pp.504-514.

14. Lahdenperä, M., Lummaa, V., Helle, S., Tremblay, M. and Russell, A.F., 2004. Fitness benefits of prolonged post-reproductive lifespan in women. Nature, 428(6979), pp.178-181.

CHAPTER 4
Global Cooling and the Last Glacial Maximum

THE WARMER AND DRIER CLIMATE in East Africa over the last five million years turned out to be disastrous for dozens of archaic species including saber-toothed tigers and several species of elephants, pigs, bovids, and monkeys. The environmental stresses accompanying the regional warming were just too much for them and they slipped into extinction. Those same stresses created new ecological niches that could be exploited by new species, several of which were hominins that eventually led to *Homo sapiens*.

So how could a species, specifically adapted to the hot, arid and dry conditions of East Africa (bipedal locomotion, loss of fur, perspiration-based cooling), endure the bitterly cold conditions they encountered as they migrated into Eurasia during the ice ages? The relatively short duration of the individual glacial maximums (5,000 to 20,000 years) (Figure 4.1) would preclude massive evolutionary adjustment to those conditions. Yet endure the cold they did, and in some cases they even thrived. The archeological evidence for humans living under extremely cold conditions is overwhelming, and it culminates with humans migrating from Eurasia to America after the most recent glacial maximum.

The definition of an invasive species is one that is "an introduced organism that negatively alters its new environment." By that definition, humans certainly qualify as an invasive species. The only difference is that we have done the introducing ourselves, as opposed to an

Ice Age Temperature Changes

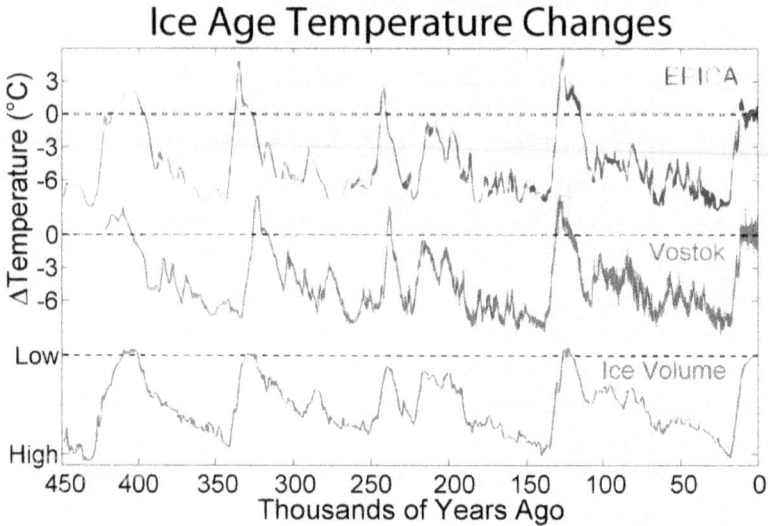

Figure 4.1. Temperature changes and ice volume associated with glacial advances and retreats over the last 450,000 years compiled from the EPICA and Vostok ice cores in Antarctica, Source: CC BY-SA 3.0, https://commons.wikimedia.org/w/index.php?curid=466270

insect stowing away on a boat or airliner. In fact, our tendency for being invasive seems to be basic human behavior as we've "introduced" ourselves into just about every part of planet Earth. One can argue that our presence often has negatively altered our environment vis-à-vis all the other species we've driven into extinction. In any case, while all hominins originally evolved in Africa, by 1.8 million years ago one hominin (*Homo erectus*) had migrated out of Africa and had reached central Europe. From there, *Homo erectus* spread out over all of Eurasia and by 1.6 million years had reached China (the so-called Peking Man) and Indonesia (the so-called Java Man).

After fully modern humans arrived on the scene about 100,000 years ago, they left Africa in several waves of migration that seem to have been made possible by climate change. The only way to migrate out of Africa is to somehow traverse what is now the Sahara Desert. One possibility is to follow the Nile River from what is now Ethiopia to the Mediterranean Sea and take a left-hand turn through what is now Israel. But the Sahara Desert was not always a desert. We've already seen how the climate of East Africa changed over the last five million years and how that change drove the evolution of hominins. It turns out that orbital processes, particularly the ~20-million-year equinox precession cycle, cause the Sahara to periodically become cooler and wetter.[1] This change, in turn, makes migrating out of Africa to Eurasia much easier for humans. As many as five waves of human migrations out of Africa (which seem to correlate with various indicators of climate change) have occurred over the last 100,000 years.[2]

Just as interesting, genetic differences between modern human populations (as indicated by single-nucleotide polymorphisms (SNPs)) reflect those human migrations to this day. SNPs are small genetic differences between individuals in a given breeding population that accumulate over time. Human populations that have been interbreeding for longer periods of time have more SNPs than populations interbreeding for shorter periods of time. Modern human populations located within Africa exhibit the highest SNP diversity (75%) whereas Native American populations, the most geographically removed from Africa, exhibit the least (50%). The rest the of world's populations are scattered somewhere in between these percentages.[3]

Beginning about 100,000 years ago, not long before the first waves of human migrations out of Africa began, global temperatures cooled, culminating in the last glacial maximum 20,000 years ago (Figure 4.1). With glaciers covering most of Western Europe at the maximum, those humans didn't have much choice but to migrate south ahead of the ice. In addition to being cold, the weather of both North America and Europe was fairly humid, leading to the accumulation and movement of thick continental glaciers. Conditions were different in Eastern Eurasia, particularly in what is now Siberia. It was cold, much colder than it is today, but it was also relatively dry. While ice accumulated in some places, much of the landscape consisted of ice-free tundra and cold grasslands. The Siberian tundra had abundant grasses and cold-adapted lichens that supported populations of mammoth, bison, reindeer, and other large mammals. Those game animals were an attractive source of food for human hunter gatherers,[4] assuming those humans could endure the cold weather. The only way to endure was with technological innovations, and they developed some sophisticated ones.

An archeological site located near Lake Baikal in southern Siberia, Mal'ta, has yielded hundreds of artifacts illustrating that technology.[5] It begins with the weapons needed to hunt large game animals like bison and reindeer. Pointed weapons kill by causing their prey to bleed to death. Although hominins had been making spear points out of chert and obsidian for more than two million years, it's difficult to hone a sharp-edged spear point capable of causing a lot of bleeding. The inhabitants of Mal'ta solved that problem by using what is called microblade technology. By carefully preparing a wedge-shaped "core" of chert, it was possible to split off flakes that were typically twice as long as they were wide. More importantly, those flakes had much sharper edges, resulting in very lethal spear points. Hundreds of these microblades have been found at Siberian archeology sites. Also found at those sites are the bones of bison, red deer, reindeer, rhinoceros, and mammoths, as well as foxes, wolves, and lions. Clearly, meat was the principal item in the diet of these people.

Another advantage the people who inhabited Siberia had during the glacial maximum was, ironically enough, the bitter cold itself. One problem with hunting large mammals such as bison or elk is preserving the meat before it spoils. During the glacial maximum, meat preservation wasn't a problem. A family could kill two or three bison in the autumn, cut up the meat in meal-size chunks, and simply let it freeze.

Once frozen, the meat couldn't spoil. It's entirely possible that a family could eat reasonably well for the whole winter having procured just a few kills. We tend to think that really cold weather would make life really hard. When it came to making a living on the Siberian Steppe, however, cold weather may have been integral to the people's survival.

Scholars debate whether the largest and most formidable of those animals, the mammoths and rhinoceros, were routinely hunted or whether they were mainly scavenged. Regardless, the bones of those large animals were used to form the walls of semi-subterranean houses covered with animal skins that could protect the inhabitants from the harsh elements of the Siberian weather. Other artifacts found at Mal'ta were figurines carved out of bone or ivory that clearly show that the people wore sophisticated clothing made from animal hides (Figure 4.2).

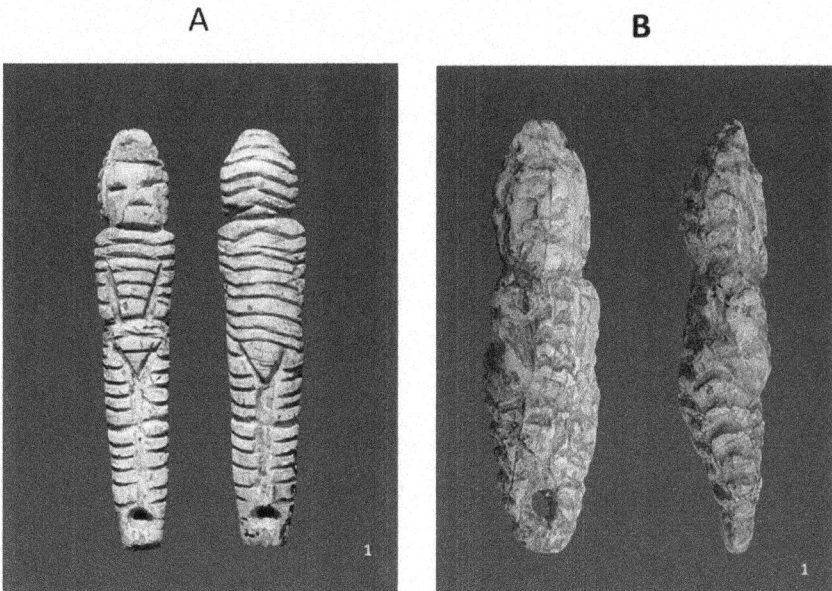

Figure 4.2. Figurines showing (A) adult and (B) child/baby clothing found at Mal'ta, Siberia. Reproduced from Lbova 2021[5], an open source journal.

Also found at the site were needles equipped with eyeholes for the tight stitching that would be needed to keep out the arctic chill. In addition to the clothed figurines, figurines of nude women were also found at Mal'ta notable for their exaggerated breasts and buttocks. These have been variously interpreted as images of fertility goddesses or other objects of worship. They may simply have been made by lonely hunters who missed their wives while they were away hunting.

The technology exhibited by the people of Mal'ta is important for another reason in human history: it enabled the ancestral Siberians to migrate to North America about 13,000 years ago, just as the Last Glacial Maximum was ending. According to DNA studies[3], the Siberians who did not migrate to America became ancestral to the modern Yakut people still living in Siberia, and the Daur and Oroqen people of Mongolia.

What was life like for those Siberian hunter gatherers? Thanks to a graveyard discovered at a place called Khuzhir-Nuge XIV on the western shore of Lake Baikal in Siberia containing seventy-nine graves with eighty-nine burials, we can glimpse what those people ate, something of their social organization, and how much they moved around during their lives.[5] The dates of these Early Bronze Age burials (about 2700-2000 BCE) were well after the Last Glacial Maximum. Much of the technology they used was similar to what had been used at Mal'ta.

This study by Andrzej Weber and colleagues[6] is also interesting because it is based on the stable isotopes of strontium ($^{87}Sr/^{86}Sr$), carbon ($^{13}C/^{12}C$), and nitrogen ($^{15}N/^{14}N$) in the bones and teeth recovered from the burials. The ratios of those isotopes in our bodies reflect the isotopic composition of what we eat. If one can figure out the isotopic composition of different foods, one can estimate what foods a person has eaten during their lifetime. When that person dies, the isotopic composition of teeth and bones is a semi-permanent record of what the person ate. Furthermore, because the enamel in teeth develops at different times during childhood, it can also be a record of how their diet changed over time.

The people living in Siberia during the early Bronze Age had just three potential food sources. The first source was game, such as deer, reindeer, and rabbits, etc. The second source was fish, including perch, pike, whitefish, and grayling. The third source was the seals that lived in Lake Baikal during the early Bronze Age as they still do today. The fish in the rivers and lakes of Siberia have a higher $^{15}\delta N$ (the ratio of $^{15}N/^{14}N$ relative to a standard) signature than the available game animals. Furthermore, because the seals eat fish, seals have an even higher $^{15}\delta N$ signature than the fish. Based solely on the nitrogen and carbon isotopes, Weber and colleagues deduced that the diets of people buried in the cemeteries fell into two groups. One group subsisted on just game and fish (GF), and the other on game, fish, and seals (GFS). Different diets imply different lifestyles, so here was evidence not only about people's diet but also about their social organization.

That brings us back to the stable isotopes of strontium. Because the atomic mass of strontium-87 and strontium-86 are virtually identical, they both have similar chemical properties. There is little or no fractionation between the two isotopes when strontium undergoes chemical or biological reactions. Furthermore, because calcium sits just above strontium on the periodic table, the chemical properties of strontium are very similar to calcium. The human body builds teeth and bones with calcium, but a certain amount of strontium can substitute for calcium as well. The ratio of strontium to calcium in human bones ranges from 1:1,000 to 1:2,000.

So how does this information help an archeologist? Different rock types have different ratios of the strontium isotopes ^{87}Sr and ^{86}Sr. Furthermore, the plants growing on soils derived from different kinds of rock, and thus the bones of the animals eating those plants, have the same $^{87}Sr/^{86}Sr$ as the rocks. Because rock types vary geographically, the $^{87}Sr/^{86}Sr$ ratios in human bones and teeth can tell an archeologist where a person grew up and if that person died in a place different from where they grew up. Strontium isotopes, therefore, can indicate patterns of human migration, presuming that archeologists can find a cemetery with almost a hundred human burials.

The geology of Siberia is particularly well-suited to using the $^{87}Sr/^{86}Sr$ method in archeology. The rocks underlying much of Siberia are either very ancient Proterozoic (more than a billion years old), moderately ancient lower Paleozoic (300,000 to 500,000 years old), less ancient Mesozoic (100,000 to 200,000), or very recent (~10,000). Furthermore, each rock type has distinct $^{87}Sr/^{86}Sr$ ratios. For those people who lived most of their lives in or near Khuzhir-Nuge XIV on Lake Baikal, their $^{87}Sr/^{86}Sr$ ratios ranged from 0.712 to 0.717. For people who came from outside that area, the ratios were distinctly lower and ranged from 0.708 to 0.712. Based on this information, archeologists concluded that about half of the burials in Khuzhir-Nuge XIV were local people, and about half had migrated from surrounding areas. This conclusion suggests that the locals and non-locals were integrated into a cohesive micro-regional group, implying a degree of cooperation between Khuzhir-Nuge XIV locals and the probably migratory non-locals. In other words, the isotopic data suggests that social cooperation, in addition to technological sophistication, was one of the human solutions for dealing with the ambient cold climate.

The global cooling that culminated in the Last Glacial Maximum, while certainly being uncomfortable for the humans living in Eurasia, was not the disaster that accompanied global cooling following the 1257 CE eruption of the Samalas volcano in Indonesia (chapter 1). The obvious difference between the two cooling episodes is one of timing. The Samalas eruption occurred over months, the cooling effect on the world's climate became noticeable about a year later, and those effects were felt for about a decade. The global cooling that culminated with the Last Glacial Maximum, on the other hand, occurred over roughly 100,000 years, permitting humans plenty of time to adapt to the changing conditions. Those humans living in Western Europe adapted by retreating from the advancing continental glaciers. Those humans living in the drier northeastern Europe and Asia who didn't have to deal with widespread continental glaciers largely remained where they were. As we've seen, they adapted in part by developing sophisticated cold-weather technologies and cooperative social interactions.

The archeology of Siberia clearly shows that, given the time to adapt, humans were perfectly capable of long-term survival in one of the coldest climates on earth. That capability proved to be a genetic boon to those Siberians crossing the Bering Sea land bridge to North America as the last ice age began to end 13,000 years ago. After reaching North America, those Siberians spread out and, as the saying goes, were fertile and multiplied. It is estimated that when Columbus arrived in 1492 CE, the population of "natives" in the Americas could have been as high as 112 million. Like the global cooling and regional warming that drove the evolution of hominins in Africa over the last five million years (chapter 3), climate change during the last glacial maximum turned out to be a huge genetic positive for the Siberians who first colonized the Americas.

REFERENCES

1. Castañeda, I.S., Mulitza, S., Schefuß, E., dos Santos, R.A.L., Damsté, J.S.S. and Schouten, S., 2009. Wet phases in the Sahara/Sahel region and human migration patterns in North Africa. Proceedings of the National Academy of Sciences, 106(48), pp.20159-20163.

2. Timmermann, A. and Friedrich, T., 2016. Late Pleistocene climate drivers of early human migration. Nature, 538(7623), pp.92-95.

3. Li, J.Z., Absher, D.M., Tang, H., Southwick, A.M., Casto, A.M., Ramachandran, S., Cann, H.M., Barsh, G.S., Feldman, M., Cavalli-Sforza, L.L. and Myers, R.M., 2008. Worldwide human relationships inferred from genome-wide patterns of variation. Science, 319(5866), pp.1100-1104.

4. Kuzmin, Y.V., 2008. Siberia at the Last Glacial Maximum: environment and archaeology. Journal of Archaeological Research, 16(2), pp.163-221.

5. Lbova, L., 2021. The Siberian Paleolithic site of Mal'ta: a unique source for the study of childhood archaeology. Evolutionary Human Sciences, 3.

6. Weber, A.W. and Goriunova, O.I., 2013. Hunter–gatherer migrations, mobility and social relations: A case study from the Early Bronze Age Baikal region, Siberia. Journal of Anthropological Archaeology, 32(3), pp.330-346.

CHAPTER 5
What Caused the Ice Ages?

JOHANN WOLFGANG VON GOETHE (1749-1832) is widely considered to be Germany's national poet, and he is certainly one of the most important writers of the German language. His most famous work, a tragic drama in two parts entitled "Faust," has been termed "*the* drama of the German people." Published in 1808, the play revolves around a bargain in which the devil agrees to give Faust everything he wants in this life in exchange for serving the devil in hell for eternity. Predictably, this bargain results in Faust seducing a beautiful maiden, a subsequent unwanted pregnancy, and various kinds of murders for which the maiden (not Faust) is ultimately condemned to death. The tragedy is that the innocent maiden pays the price for Faust's sin. By all accounts, the poetic language in German is hauntingly beautiful. It is unfortunate that that beauty does not translate easily into English, and thus Goethe's poetry is less well known in the English-speaking world. But in addition to being a famous and revered poet, Goethe was also an avid geologist. As such, he had a share in the discovery that glaciers once covered much of Germany during what we now call the ice ages.[1]

At the age of twenty-six, and on the strength of his first great literary success (a 1774 novel entitled *The Sorrows of Young Werther*), Goethe was offered and accepted employment by the Duke of Saxe-Weimar-Eisenach. Promptly appointed to the Duke's Mines and Highways Commission, Goethe oversaw the reopening of a silver mine.

This experience led to his lifelong interest in geology in general and mineralogy in particular. When he died in 1832, Goethe possessed one of the largest private mineral collections in Europe. In recognition of his contributions to mineralogy, the rusty-colored iron mineral with the (approximate) chemical formula $FeO(OH)$ was named *goethite* in his honor.

Goethe's role in the discovery of the ice ages was less straightforward. For centuries, people had noticed the presence of unusual and mysterious very large rocks (some as big as a house) strewn across the plains of northern Germany (Fig. 5.1).

Figure 5.1. A typical Erratic Boulder. Note that the boulder is a different rock type than the underlying bedrock: U.S. Geological Survey file photo.

These rocks, known as "erratics," were clearly different than the underlying sediments or bedrock. It was also noticed that erratics in northern Germany were identical in composition to rocks found in

Scandinavia, hundreds of kilometers away. What could possibly have moved them? As it happens, Goethe was also familiar with granite erratics found in Austria and Switzerland, which some local mountaineers claimed had been moved by glaciers. Goethe surmised that glaciers had transported the erratics plainly visible in the Alps. Goethe wrote:[1]

> *The glaciers travel through the valleys to the edge of the lake carrying the granite blocks loosed from above, as still happens today. The blocks remain on the lake plain after the ice melts, to be found today, unrounded, because they were brought there smoothly, and not forcefully.*

Based on that quotation, penned about 1792, one could reasonably conclude that Goethe was the first person to attribute the presence of erratics to the movement of glaciers.[1] However, that very same idea had been previously published in 1787 by B.F. Kuhn.[2] Did Goethe get the idea from Kuhn, or did Goethe simply come to the same conclusion independently? In many ways it really doesn't matter because (at least in the short run) Kuhn's and Goethe's idea went nowhere. Most people were simply unaware of what they were saying, and if they were aware, they either dismissed it outright or simply ignored it. The day of the glaciers had not yet arrived.

Yet the basic evidence—the ubiquitous presence of erratic boulders all over northern Europe—was almost impossible to ignore. One of the people who didn't ignore their presence was a Swiss engineer named Ignaz Venetz who, in 1816, was working high in the Alps attempting to drain an ice-dammed lake. He didn't succeed in that endeavor (the dam failed catastrophically in 1818), but he did observe that the valley displayed clear evidence that it had been carved by a glacier that had subsequently retreated. In 1821, Venetz wrote a paper suggesting that the climate in Switzerland had once been much colder and that much of the land had been covered with ice.

About the same time, a Swiss geologist named Jean de Charpentier (an acquaintance of Venetz) happened to be traveling in the Alps. As there were no hotels, de Charpentier spent a night in the cottage of a local mountaineer. In conversation, the mountaineer casually mentioned that the glaciers present at higher elevations used to extend much further down the valleys. The mountaineer said, "I find huge boulders of alpine granite perched on the sides of the valleys, where they could only have been left by ice."[3] That captured de Charpentier's attention, and he spent several years investigating the geologic evidence that glaciers could move huge boulders out of the Alps and into the surrounding valleys. In 1834, de Charpentier read a paper to the Association of Swiss Naturalists summarizing the evidence he and Venetz had collected, proposing that in the past, much of Switzerland must have been covered by glaciers. Predictably, these ideas were met with skepticism, but they intrigued one scientist in attendance: Louis Agassiz.[3]

Agassiz was understandably skeptical of what de Charpentier had to say but was willing to investigate the matter himself. With de Charpentier as a guide, Agassiz spent the summer of 1836 examining the glacial terrain near Bex, Switzerland, where de Charpentier directed the local salt mine. Agassiz was soon convinced that Venetz and de Charpentier were right, and he immediately understood the implications for the geology of not just Switzerland, but all of Europe as well. Importantly, Agassiz was very much part of the European scientific establishment of the day, having studied paleontology with Georges Cuvier and medicine with Alexander von Humboldt in Paris. So, when Agassiz read a paper to the Helvetic society in 1837, essentially repeating what Khun, Goethe, Venetz, and de Charpentier had said earlier, it lent considerable weight to the argument. In addition to his scientific stature, Agassiz's original contribution was recognizing that glaciers could not only explain the landscape of Switzerland, but also the erratics found in northern Germany. Furthermore, Agassiz proposed that, in the relatively recent geologic past, most of Europe had been covered by a vast ice sheet, a time which Agassiz called the *Eiszeit* or "ice age."[4] Agassiz published these findings in 1837, which was after Venetz had published his book in 1833 and before de Charpentier published his findings in 1840. In any case, once these publications were available, geologists across the world began to recognize evidence for ice ages.

Immediately the question was what caused ice ages, and just as importantly, what ended them. The first person to address that question was the French mathematician Joseph Adhémar (1797–1862) in his 1842 book *Revolutions of the Sea*. It's remarkable that that book was published just a few years after the Venetz, Agassiz, and de Charpentier papers, but it reflects the intense interest their contemporaries had in the ice age hypothesis. Adhémar proposed that glacial and interglacial periods were controlled by astronomical factors. Specifically, he pointed out that in the northern hemisphere, the earth is closest to the sun at the winter solstice. Because the earth's orbital velocity is faster when closer to the sun, the time between the autumn Equinox to the winter solstice is shorter than the period from the spring equinox to the summer solstice by about seven days. The opposite is true in the southern hemisphere. He claimed that at the present day, ice should currently be accumulating more in the southern hemisphere and less in the northern hemisphere. That, of course, will reverse in approximately 20,000 years due to the precession of the equinoxes. For that reason, he suggested a periodicity of 20,000 years for ice ages in the northern hemisphere.

Adhémar's hypothesis was taken up by a self-taught amateur naturalist named James Croll. In the 1860s, Croll worked as a lowly janitor in the museum of the Andersonian University in Glasgow, Scotland (now the University of Strathclyde). It was a poorly paid position, but it gave him access to the school's library, which he used to teach himself astronomy and physics. Croll was aware of Agassiz's theory of the ice ages and probably of Adhémar's suggestion that their periodicity was astronomically controlled. In 1864, which actually predated the universal acceptance that ice ages had even happened, Croll published a paper arguing that the eccentricity of the earth's orbit, in combination with the precession of the equinoxes, could trigger what he called a "glacial epoch."[5] He argued that when the northern hemisphere was tilted away from the sun in the winter (the opposite of what is occurring now) with the earth's orbit at its most elliptical (which takes it farther from the sun), the amount of solar radiation reaching the earth's surface decreases. The result? Winters would be colder in the northern hemisphere, thus "triggering" an ice age. He theorized that once ice and snow accumulated in northern latitudes, more sunlight would be reflected into space (albedo), creating even more cooling. He also suggested that this cooling might cause the Gulf Stream to be diverted southward, leading to even more cooling. In concert, the combination of an astronomical "trigger" mechanism with the resulting positive feedback loops (albedo, ocean current modulation) could explain the ice ages in the northern hemisphere. Croll used the planetary orbital equations developed by Urbain Le Verrier (equations that predicted the existence of the planet Neptune) to show how astronomical precession cycles could lead to cycles of ice ages.

Croll's hypothesis was initially received positively by the geological community, which led Charles Lyell to include Croll's ice age theories in a new edition of Lyell's classic textbook *Principles of Geology*. In addition, Croll was offered and accepted a position with the Scottish office of the British Geological Survey. No more janitoring for James

Croll. He summarized his ideas about orbital processes and ice ages in his book *Climate and Time, in Their Geological Relations*, published in 1875. In recognition of that work, Croll was elected as a Fellow of the Royal Society in 1876.

After his death in 1890, Croll's work fell out of favor because age-dating techniques hadn't yet progressed to the point where the many different glacier advances and retreats he suggested could be accurately dated. Furthermore, Croll had estimated that the last ice advance had ended 80,000 years ago. The recession of Niagara Falls, however, suggested that the last ice age ended between 6,000 and 35,000 years ago. By the early 1900s, Croll's theories had been largely discounted.

$$\Longleftrightarrow$$

This was not the honeymoon that Milutin Milanković hoped for or expected. On June 14, 1914, he married Kristina Topuzović, and for their honeymoon they visited Milanković's home village of Dalj, which prior to World War I was part of the Austro-Hungarian Empire. The couple arrived at Dalj in late June with plans to spend the entire summer there. But on June 28 a Serbian named Gavrilo Princip assassinated the Austro-Hungarian heir Archduke Franz Ferdinand in Sarajevo. By July, Serbia and the Austro-Hungarian Empire were on the verge of war. Because Milanković was a Serbian national, he was promptly arrested and thrown into jail. Milanković later remembered:

> *The heavy iron door closed behind me....I sat on my bed, looked around the room and started to take in my new social circumstances... In my hand luggage which I brought with me were my already printed or only started works on my cosmic problem; there was even some blank paper. I looked over my works, took my faithful ink pen and started to write and calculate.*

It turns out that Milanković was fortunate in the choice of his new wife. She traveled to Vienna, the capital of Austro-Hungarian Empire, and met with one of Milanković's former professors. Through the professor's connections, she managed to get Milanković released from jail and obtained permission for him to spend his captivity in Budapest. Upon arriving there, Milanković met with the Director of the Library of the Hungarian Academy of Science, who happened to be a mathematician. The director was delighted to have Milanković in Budapest and gave him full access to the library and to the Hungarian Central Meteorological Institute. For the rest of the war, Milanković *took his faithful ink pen and started to write and calculate.*

Milanković had been trained as an engineer and had learned some advanced mathematics as well. While in Budapest, he applied those mathematics to investigate the climate of the inner planets of the solar system, developing methods for estimating the surface temperature of those planets based on the incidence of solar radiation. In 1916, he published a paper entitled *Investigation of the climate of Mars* in which he estimated the average surface temperature of Mars to be -17° C.

He then applied those mathematical techniques to the climate of the earth. In particular, he investigated variations in solar radiation due to the changing elliptical orbit of the earth (eccentricity), the tilt of the earth's spin axis (obliquity), and the wobble in the earth's spin axis (precession of the equinoxes). Because each of these phenomena operate on different time scales (eccentricity~100,000 years, obliquity~41,000 years, precession~20,000 years), their effects on insolation vary continuously over time. Milanković calculated that the insolation reaching the northern hemisphere varied by as much as 20%, depending on how the three cycles interact. For example, when the earth's orbit is at its most elliptical (farther away from the sun) and the northern hemisphere is tilted away from the sun, the climate would cool and allow ice to accumulate. Conversely, if the orbit is more circular (closer to the sun) and the northern hemisphere is tilted toward the sun (as it is now), the climate would warm.

In many ways, Milanković was repeating the concepts that had first been worked out by Adhémar and Croll. But Milanković placed those concepts on a firm mathematical foundation. When he first became interested in climate, Milanković was surprised and dismayed at the mathematical underpinnings of meteorological science in the early twentieth century, commenting:

> *most of meteorology is nothing but a collection of*
> *innumerable empirical findings, mainly numerical data,*
> *with traces of physics used to explain some of them…*
> *Mathematics was even less applied, nothing more than*
> *elementary calculus… advanced mathematics had no role*
> *in that science….*

One detail of Milanković's theory differed from Croll's in a significant way. While Croll had thought that the increasing coldness of the winter months led to an ice age, Milanković thought that the increasing coldness of the *summer* months in high latitudes kept winter snow from melting completely in the summer. As snow accumulated over time, more and more solar radiation would be reflected into space, causing accelerated cooling. After many thousands of years, the snow cover solidifies into a glacier that moves and pushes southward.[6]

Initially, Milanković's theory was welcomed by the scientific community, largely because it gave a plausible explanation for the many successive ice ages that had happened over the last 2.4 million years. But soon it became evident that Milanković's theory suffered from the same problem as Adhémar's and Croll's theories: no hard geologic evidence could either corroborate or refute it. Dating successive ice ages using the sedimentological record is problematic, largely because each ice advance tends to gouge out and erase sediments left by previous ice advances. One possible answer to this dilemma was something that James Croll had suggested a hundred years before. He suspected that sediments deposited on the sea floor could provide a continuous record of how ocean temperatures had changed over time. Specifically, he proposed that cold or warm-water planktonic microorganisms might be used as temperature-indicator species.

That suggestion is ultimately what happened, albeit in ways that Croll could not have anticipated. Shortly after World War II, Sweden sent out the oceanographic research vessel *Albatross* equipped with a piston-coring rig capable of retrieving from the ocean bottom sediment cores of up to fifteen meters in length. Between 1947 and 1948, the crew of the *Albatross* collected about 300 cores of sediments, eight of which were sampled for planktonic foraminiferal tests (that is, shells), which could then be analyzed for their $^{18}O/^{16}O$ ratios. Because the fractionation of the two stable isotopes of oxygen (^{18}O and ^{16}O) during the growth of foraminiferal tests is temperature dependent, Cesare Emiliani proposed that $^{18}O/^{16}O$ ratios could act as a thermometer capturing ocean temperatures in the past[7]. He was partially right. The more important process in determining the $^{18}O/^{16}O$ composition of sea water is due to simple evaporation. Because ^{18}O is heavier than ^{16}O, water composed of ^{16}O evaporates more readily than that composed of ^{18}O. During ice ages, much of that ^{16}O water vapor fell as snow in higher latitudes and was trapped in glaciers. Thus, during ice ages, the amount of ^{18}O in seawater increased. Conversely, when the glaciers melted, the ^{18}O composition of seawater decreased.[8]

The $^{18}O/^{16}O$ record derived from deep-sea cores gives a remarkably detailed view of changing oceanic temperatures over the last two million years (Figure 5.2) and, by extension, the cycles of the advances and retreats of continental glaciers[9]. The question is, do the glacial cycles match the cycles of eccentricity, obliquity, and precession? As things stand today, the answer is a qualified "maybe."

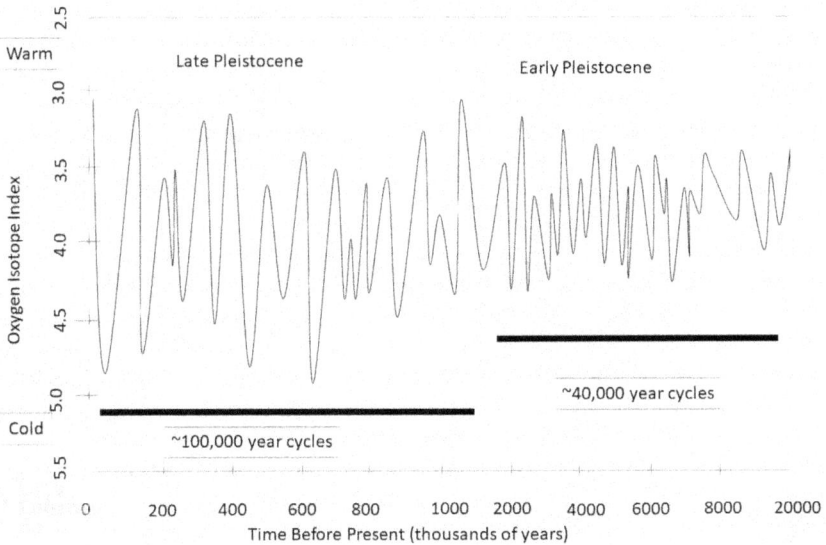

Figure 5.2. Ice-age cycles of the last two million years, as indicated by the δ^{18}O values of benthic foraminifera from deep-sea sediments. Data is from Berger et al., 2010[9].

In 1976, a team led by James Hays at Columbia University used an ^{18}O/^{16}O record derived from deep-sea cores over the past 500,000 years and, using a variety of curve-smoothing techniques, uncovered evidence for regular glacial cycles of 21,000 (precession) and 41,000 (obliquity) years.[8] The researchers observed evidence of a strong 100,000-year cycle (eccentricity) as well, a puzzling finding because eccentricity has a much weaker effect on insolation than obliquity and precession. A later study by a team headed by Wolfang Berger of the Scripps Institute also saw evidence of both 41,000- and 100,000-year cycles but not 20,000.[9]

The glacial cycles in the early part of the Pleistocene had a periodicity of about 40,000 years, as indicated by Fourier analysis (Fig. 5.2)[9]. That periodicity would be consistent with the insolation cycles predicted by obliquity. In the late Pleistocene, however, the cycles had a periodicity of closer to 100,000 years. Also, there was a marked decrease in the average temperature between the early and late Pleistocene, possibly reflecting the 100,000-year insolation cycle predicted by eccentricity. The problem with that interpretation, again, is that eccentricity is supposed to have a smaller effect on solar insolation relative to obliquity and precession. Finally, where is the evidence (Fig. 5.2) for a 20,000-year cycle?

Maureen Raymo of Columbia University and colleagues suggested one possible explanation for the apparent lack of a clear signal for precession (~20,000 years) in the $^{18}O/^{16}O$ record.[10] They posited that between three and one million years ago, ice volume changes occurred in both the Northern and Southern Hemispheres, each controlled by local summer solar radiation. Because Earth's precession is 180 degrees out of phase between the two hemispheres, 20,000-year changes in ice volume in each hemisphere could have cancelled out the signal from globally integrated proxies such as ocean $^{18}O/^{16}O$ ratios, leaving the in-phase obliquity (41,000 years) component of insolation to dominate those records.

The cycles in the early Pleistocene are also characterized by less extreme temperature changes than those in the late Pleistocene (Fig. 5.2). Again, nobody knows why. Nonetheless, several important conclusions can be drawn from this record. For one, the glacial advances and retreats operate on time frames of tens of thousands of years. In the late Pleistocene, it's been estimated that it took close to 90,000 years for the ice sheets to fully form. The last glacial maximum ended about 20,000 years ago, and the retreat of the ice sheets in North America and Europe was largely completed by 8,000 years ago. It took a long time for the last ice age to develop, and a good deal less time for the warming that melted the ice.

So, are the observed 100,000- and 40,000-year cycles in the $^{18}O/^{16}O$ record consistent with Milanković's predictions of a 100,000-year cycle (eccentricity) and a 40,000-year cycle (obliquity)? Possibly. The 100,000-year periodicity predicted by Milanković in 1930 is virtually identical to the record of the late Pleistocene (Fig. 5.2). Furthermore, the 41,000-year cycle of the early Pleistocene certainly is strong evidence of the importance of obliquity, but there's no definitive proof.

Today, most researchers accept that orbital "forcing" by eccentricity, obliquity, and precession are involved with initiating glacial episodes and perhaps involved with ending them. Superimposed on orbital processes are the effects of volcanic, ocean currents, and atmospheric processes that interact with orbital processes in ways that are difficult to imagine, much less predict. We can conclude, however, that because of these interactions, it's simply not realistic to make meaningful predictions concerning the timing of future warming and cooling cycles.[9]

However, the geologic evidence shows that warm interglacial periods, such as what we have experienced for all of written human history, will at some point end and the climate will cool once more.

REFERENCES

1. Cameron, D., 1964. Early discoverers XXII, Goethe-Discoverer of the ice age. Journal of Glaciology 5(41): 751-754.

2. Kuhn, B.F. 1787. Versuch uber den mechanismus der Gletscher. A Hopfrers fur die Naturkunde Helvetiens (Zurich). 1, pp. 119-136. (Investigation into the mechanism of the glacier. A contribution for the natural history of Switzerland.

3. Marcou, J., 1886. Glaciers and glacialists. Science vol. VII, no. 181: 76-80.

4. Pering, T. 2009. The History and Philosophy of Glaciology. http://www.volcano-blog.com/uploads/6/9/7/6/6976040/the_history_and_philosophy_of_glaciology.pdf. Accessed 4-4-2017.

5. Croll, James. 1864 On the physical cause of the change of climate during geological epochs. Philosophical Magazine, 28:121-137.

6. Raymo, M.E. and Huybers, P., 2008. Unlocking the mysteries of the ice ages. Nature, 451(7176), pp.284-285.

7. Emiliani, C, 1955. Pleistocene temperatures. The Journal of Geology 63(6), pp. 538-578.

8. Hays, J.D., Imbrie, J. and Shackleton, N.J., 1976, December. Variations in the Earth's orbit: pacemaker of the ice ages. Washington, DC: American Association for the Advancement of Science.

9. Berger, W.H., Schulz, M. and Wefer, G., 2010. Quaternary oceans and climate change: lessons for the future? International Journal of Earth Sciences, 99(1), pp.171-189.

10. Raymo, M.E., Lisiecki, L.E. and Nisancioglu, K.H., 2006. Plio-Pleisto-cene ice volume, Antarctic climate, and the global $\delta^{18}O$ record. Science, 313(5786), pp.492-495.

CHAPTER 6
Warming and the Agricultural Revolution

THE EVENT IN EARTH'S HISTORY that made the agricultural revolution possible—humans domesticating plants and animals for food—happened about 15,000 years ago. That event was the sudden end (in a few decades) of the last ice age. Exactly what happened to cause this abrupt shift in the earth's climate is, of course, controversial. But it does seem that in the space of about fifty years, the average temperature encountered at the Greenland Summit warmed between 6° and 12°C.[1]

A variety of orbital, atmospheric, and oceanic reasons have been advanced to explain how and why this abrupt warming happened. From an orbital perspective, a confluence of the earth's obliquity (tilt of earth's rotation axis) and the precession of the equinoxes (the wobble in earth's spin)[2] increased the solar energy reaching the northern hemisphere.[3] That confluence led to the breakup of the northern glaciers, which delivered sea ice and cold water to the north Atlantic. That colder water produced changes in both oceanic and atmospheric circulation patterns that pushed warmer water to Antarctica, causing warming in the southern hemisphere as well. Those warming patterns were accompanied by increased atmospheric greenhouse gas concentrations (water vapor, carbon dioxide, and methane), trapping additional solar energy in the atmosphere and accelerating the warming trend. The "trigger" most probably caused by the fortuitous aligning of orbital obliquity and precession began a cascade of oceanic and atmospheric changes that ended the last ice age. Similar events seem also to have caused the "terminations" of the twenty or so glacial advances (Fig. 5.2) that had occurred over the last two and a half million years.[1,2,3] Regardless of the precise reasons, the incontrovertible fact is that between 15,000 and 10,000 years ago, the earth's climate warmed considerably and entered an interglacial period that continues to this day.

This global warming is what made plant agriculture possible in much of the world. Figure 6.1 shows the extent of the ice covering northern Europe 20,000 years ago before warming began, and the ice extent 9,500 years ago. By 9,500 years ago, Britain was ice-free, as was most of northern Europe except for Scandinavia. The first evidence of agriculture in Europe, however, dates to approximately 7,500 years ago.[4] It took another 4,000 years after Europe was largely ice-free for humans to invent agriculture in the Middle East and then for it to spread westward.

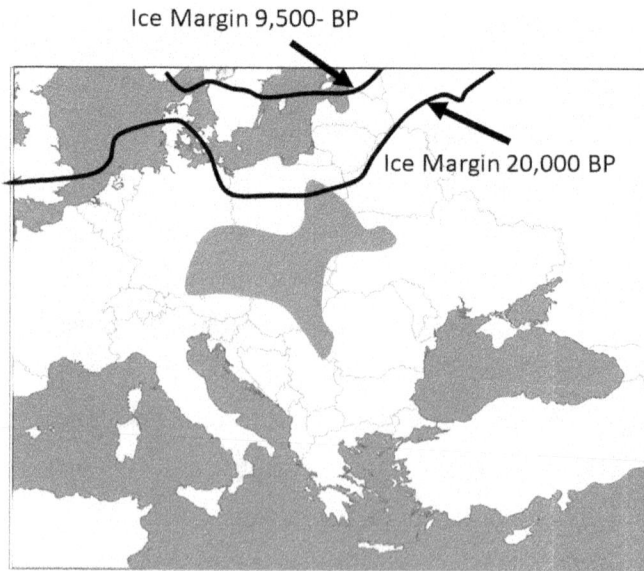

Figure. 6.1. The green shading shows the first farming areas in central Europe about 5,000 BCE. Data is from Bramanti et al., 2009[4].

How the agricultural revolution came to be will probably never be known precisely. What we do know is that agriculture was invented independently in several times and places, including Southeast Asia[5], the Middle East[6], and in the Americas.[7] Why it came about is less of a mystery. The hunter-gatherer lifestyle, which had been practiced by hominins for five million years, can be terrifyingly uncertain. Any interruption of food gathering for just a few days—floods, droughts, excessive heat or cold, and about any kind of natural catastrophe—can easily lead to starvation. For civilization to be possible, humanity needed a more consistent food supply. It's a reasonable guess that need is what sparked the agricultural revolution.

If we consider the kinds of plants and animals pre-agricultural humans gathered, we can reconstruct how agriculture developed in the first place. Archeological evidence points to what sorts of plants pre-agricultural people routinely gathered and ate. One cave site in southern Spain known as Santa Maira, for example, has yielded evidence that the inhabitants gathered and ate the acorns of oak trees, grass seeds, and legumes.[8] Hominins had doubtless been eating seeds and nuts for several million years, but the earliest archeological evidence for that behavior is from only 105,000 years ago.[9] The fact that hunter-gatherers demonstrably collected seeds and acorns for food implies a knowledge of their seasonality and ultimately their mode of reproduction. Once they understood how seeds were involved in plant reproduction, plant agriculture could proceed. It does seem, however, that the first domestications were for animals, beginning with dogs between 20,000 and 40,000 years ago. Pigs and sheep were domesticated later around 8,500 BCE, and cattle somewhat later still around 6,500 BCE.

It used to be thought that plant agriculture began in the fertile crescent of the Levant (modern Syria, Lebanon, and Israel). It's now known that plant agriculture arose independently in at least eleven different places in both the Old and New World. The Levant, however, illustrates how climate change was involved with the development of plants that were eventually domesticated. As the glacial retreat proceeded in the northern hemisphere, the climate of the Levant became drier and hotter. Rain and snow fell predominantly in the winter months followed by a hot dry summer. That cold/wet-hot/dry alternation favored annual plants that could disperse their seeds at the close of the growing season. Seeds lay dormant through the cold winter and then germinated when warmth and water were available in the spring. They reached maturity during the dry summer months, and the cycle repeated. Emmer and einkorn wheat were two plant species that adopted such a reproductive strategy.

The seeds of these plants were an excellent source of carbohydrates and protein for human hunter-gatherers. Wild emmer wheat was gathered by Paleolithic people as early as 23,000 years ago in the southern Levant near the Sea of Galilee.[10] Those humans had learned that as the emmer wheat approached the time for seed dispersal, it was easy enough to go through a field with a basket and gather a portion of the seeds as they were released by the mature plant. Wild emmer wheat has a genetically controlled strategy for naturally dispersing its seeds, which involves forming an abscission scar on the husk that releases the seed with the aid of gravity, wind, and rain.[11] Because that process is genetically controlled, the plant can lose the ability for auto-dispersion by one or two gene mutations. Under natural conditions, such mutations are not advantageous for the plant, but if human harvesting takes the place of auto-dispersion, those gene mutations can be propagated and accumulate in the population. Similarly, other genetic mutations can produce larger seeds.[11] By about 10,000 years ago, humans seemed to have noticed the results of those mutations and actively encouraged them by replanting seeds that were more desirable. That process probably took many thousands of years, as it required genetic changes for emmer wheat[12] and behavioral changes for the people.[11] However that all came about, by 10,000 years ago, emmer wheat was being widely cultivated throughout the southern Lavant.[10] That cultivation was made possible by the warming and drying of the climate.

From its tentative beginnings, agriculture gradually spread northward and westward, and by 5,000 BCE, it had reached much of central Europe (Fig. 6.1). How that spreading occurred has been widely debated in archeological circles. Did hunter gatherers simply observe what the farmers were doing and copy them, or were the farmers themselves migrating out of the Middle East and bringing the new technology with them? A study based on mitochondrial DNA (mtDNA) recovered from skeletons found in ancient burials suggests the farmers were migrating from the Middle East.[13] A comparison of mtDNA recovered from late European hunter-gatherer skeletons with those from early farmers revealed that the two populations were demonstrably different. In other words, by 5,000 BCE there was little genetic interaction between the indigenous hunter-gatherers and the farming newcomers. That lack of interaction makes cultural sense. Farming and hunter-gathering require very different skill sets, both carefully handed down from parent to child. Furthermore, there would be language barriers. It's entirely understandable that there would be limited intimate contact between the indigenous and migrant human populations.

By 4,000 BCE, cereal agriculture had reached the island of Britain, and that's where the importance of climate on the practice of agriculture again enters the picture. For several hundred years, cereal agriculture was successfully practiced there, but after 3,600 BCE, evidence of cereal agriculture disappears from the archeological record for the next 800 years.[14] What might have happened to cause the retreat from cereal agriculture? One possibility is a period marked by a cooling climate.

We've seen that the global warming trend over the last 15,000 years was central to the development of agriculture beginning roughly 10,000 years ago. That being the case, what would happen if that warming trend reversed? The island of Britain, partly due to its history of deglaciation, has produced a unique set of climate records. As the glaciers melted, water collected into depressions originally gouged out by advancing ice. Those lakes gradually filled with organic matter over the millennia, and the resulting peat bogs provide a record of climate change going back 7,500 years.[15]

One peat bog in southeast Scotland known as Temple Hill Moss shows how Britain's climate has changed in the past. Specifically, the bog records nine different cycles of a cooler and wetter climate alternating with warmer and drier periods. On average, the wet-dry cycles seem to repeat every 1,100 years.[15] The most pronounced of these cooler and wetter periods commences at 3,500 BCE and coincides with the apparent disappearance of cereal agriculture for the next 800 years. That same climate disruption, known as the Mid-Holocene climatic reversal, has been documented in the Tyrolean Alps of Switzerland, and potentially at forty-four other sites worldwide.[16]

The development of agriculture famously allowed people to abandon the hunter-gatherer lifestyle and settle down on farmsteads. As agricultural technology advanced, villages, towns, and cities eventually grew up. By 2,400 BCE there were at least sixteen independent cities present in Mesopotamia and, humans being humans, they were also constantly fighting with each other. In 2,334 BCE, a particularly talented general named Sargon the Great managed to conquer most of Mesopotamia and establish the Akkadian Empire, possibly the first empire on earth. After Sargon's death in 2,279 BCE, his heirs held the Akkadian empire together for about a hundred years in what was a prosperous time. But in about 2,200 BCE, there was a marked and apparently sudden increase in the aridity of Mesopotamia, leading to a decrease in agricultural production, the abandonment of several cities, and the sudden collapse of the Akkadian Empire.[17]

The extent and timing of this changing climate was recorded in cored sediments recovered from the Gulf of Oman. Just before the Akkadian Empire collapsed, the sediments showed a marked increase in the amount of calcite and the ratio of strontium isotopes ($^{86}Sr/^{87}Sr$), both of which indicate the onset of a much drier climate in Mesopotamia (Figure 6.2).[18] The Akkadian Empire was not the only ancient culture to collapse due to the onset of a long-term drought. Other examples are the classical Maya civilization, which collapsed in about 1,000 CE, and the Peruvian Tiwanaku civilization, which collapsed at about the same time.[18]

Because ancient civilizations were so dependent on agriculture, they were highly vulnerable to climatic disruptions. It is not particularly controversial that the post-glacial warming trend over the past 15,000 years contributed to the rise of agriculture and civilizations 10,000 years ago. More controversial is the occurrence of periodic climate reversals superimposed on that overall warming trend. Explanations for what causes these reversals inevitably revert to the standard orbital, tectonic, oceanic, and atmospheric processes. But while those processes may provide plausible explanations, they do not yet enable us to predict how or when such changes may occur. Given the sudden cessation of cereal agriculture in Britain in 3,600 BCE that coincided with a cooling climate, and the later collapses of the Akkadian, Mayan, and Tiwanaku civilizations associated with prolonged droughts, it certainly makes one wonder how our own civilization would cope with similar episodes of climate change.

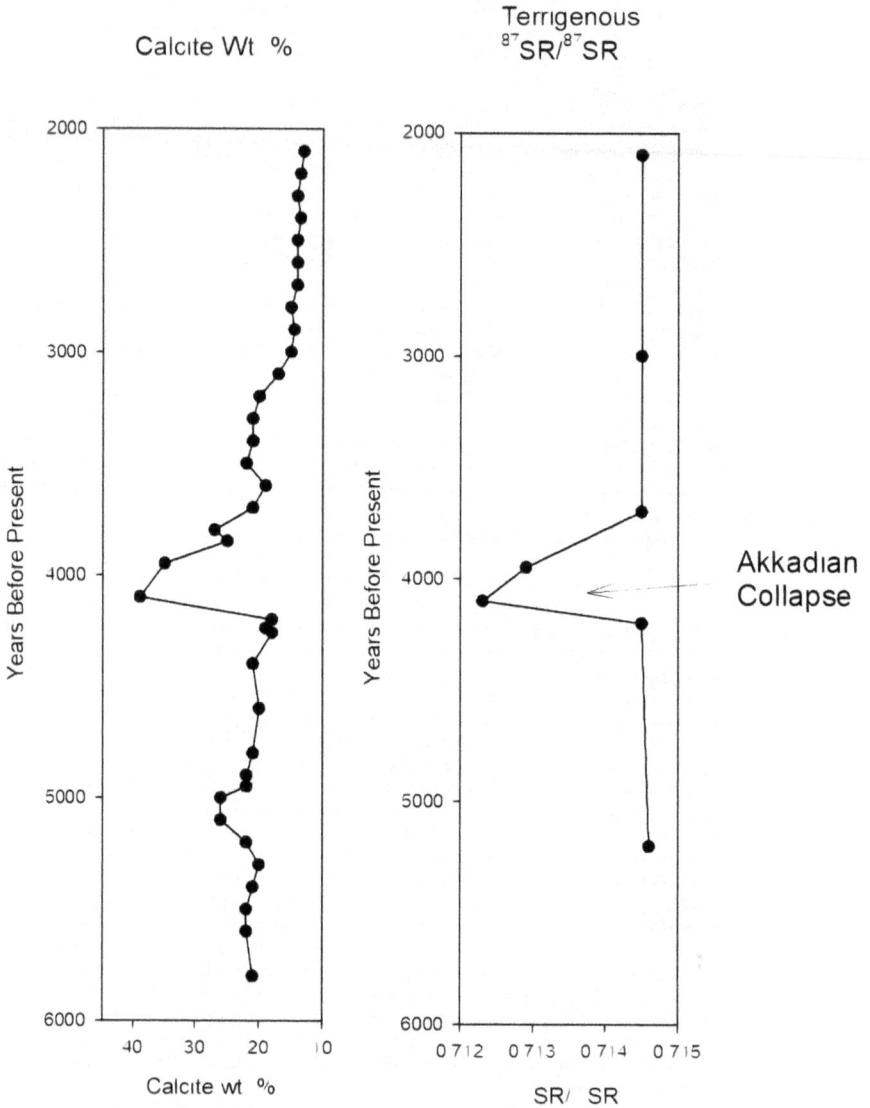

Figure 6.2. Analyses of sediment cores from the Gulf of Oman showing increased concentrations of calcite and terrigenous $^{86}Sr/^{87}Sr$ aridity in 4,200 BP and the timing of the Akkadian civilization collapse. Data is from deMenocal, 2001[18].

REFERENCES

1. Severinghaus, J.P. and Brook, E.J., 1999. Abrupt climate change at the end of the last glacial period inferred from trapped air in polar ice. Science, 286(5441), pp.930-934.

2. Bajo, P., Drysdale, R.N., Woodhead, J.D., Hellstrom, J.C., Hodell, D., Ferretti, P., Voelker, A.H., Zanchetta, G., Rodrigues, T., Wolff, E. and Tyler, J., 2020. Persistent influence of obliquity on ice age terminations since the Middle Pleistocene transition. Science, 367(6483), pp.1235-1239.

3. Cheng, H., Edwards, R.L., Broecker, W.S., Denton, G.H., Kong, X., Wang, Y., Zhang, R. and Wang, X., 2009. Ice age terminations. Science, 326(5950), pp.248-252.

4. Bramanti, B., Thomas, M.G., Haak, W., Unterländer, M., Jores, P., Tambets, K., Antanaitis-Jacobs, I., Haidle, M.N., Jankauskas, R., Kind, C.J. and Lueth, F., 2009. Genetic discontinuity between local hunter-gatherers and central Europe's first farmers. science, 326(5949), pp.137-140.

5. Solheim, W.G., 1972. An earlier agricultural revolution. Scientific American, 226(4), pp.34-41.

6. Braidwood, R.J., 1960. The agricultural revolution. Scientific American, 203(3), pp.130-152.

7. Turner II, B.L., 1974. Prehistoric intensive agriculture in the Mayan lowlands. Science, pp.118-124.

8. Aura, J.E., Carrión, Y., Estrelles, E. and Jorda, G.P., 2005. Plant economy of hunter-gatherer groups at the end of the last Ice Age: plant macroremains from the cave of Santa Maira (Alacant, Spain) ca. 12000–9000 BP. Vegetation History and Archaeobotany, 14(4), pp.542-550.

9. Mercader, J. (2009). Mozambican grass seed consumption during the Middle Stone Age. Science. 326 (5960): 1680–1683.

10. Özkan, H., Willcox, G., Graner, A., Salamini, F. and Kilian, B., 2011. Geographic distribution and domestication of wild emmer wheat (Triticum dicoccoides). Genetic resources and crop evolution, 58(1), pp.11-53.

11. Fuller, D.Q., Allaby, R.G. and Stevens, C., 2010. Domestication as innovation: the entanglement of techniques, technology and chance in the

domestication of cereal crops. World archaeology, 42(1), pp.13-28.

12. Peleg, Z., Fahima, T., Korol, A.B., Abbo, S. and Saranga, Y., 2011. Genetic analysis of wheat domestication and evolution under domestication. Journal of Experimental Botany, 62(14), pp.5051-5061.

13. Bramanti, B., Thomas, M.G., Haak, W., Unterländer, M., Jores, P., Tambets, K., Antanaitis-Jacobs, I., Haidle, M.N., Jankauskas, R., Kind, C.J. and Lueth, F., 2009. Genetic discontinuity between local hunter-gatherers and central Europe's first farmers. science, 326(5949), pp.137-140.

14. Stevens, C.J. and Fuller, D.Q., 2015. Alternative strategies to agriculture: the evidence for climatic shocks and cereal declines during the British Neolithic and Bronze Age (a reply to Bishop). World Archaeology, 47(5), pp.856-875.

15. Langdon, P.G., Barber, K.E. and Hughes, P.D.M., 2003. A 7500-year peat-based palaeoclimatic reconstruction and evidence for an 1100-year cyclicity in bog surface wetness from Temple Hill Moss, Pentland Hills, southeast Scotland. Quaternary science reviews, 22(2-4), pp.259-274.

16. Magny M, Haas JN. A major widespread climatic change around 5300 cal. yr BP at the time of the Alpine Iceman. Journal of Quaternary Science: Published for the Quaternary Research Association. 2004 Jul;19(5):423-30.

17. Weiss, H., Courty, M.A., Wetterstrom, W., Guichard, F., Senior, L., Meadow, R. and Curnow, A., 1993. The genesis and collapse of third millennium north Mesopotamian civilization. Science, 261(5124), pp.995-1004.

18. DeMenocal, P.B., 2001. Cultural responses to climate change during the late Holocene. Science, 292(5517), pp.667-673.

CHAPTER 7
Cooling and the End of the Bronze Age

IN 1450 BCE, THE CITY of Ugarit, located in what is now northern Syria, had a lot going for it. For one thing, it was a port city on the Mediterranean Sea, but even better, it was located on a crossroads leading to the cities of the Hittite Empire in what is now modern Turkey. Ugarit, therefore, was perfectly positioned as a trading center between Egypt and the city of Hattusa, the capital of the Hittites. Politically, Ugarit was alternately under Egyptian or Hittite sway depending on which kingdom was militarily ascendant. Either way, by 1450 BCE, Ugarit was one of the wealthiest cities in the Middle East. However, that all ended in 1192 BCE when the city was attacked by seven ships, was sacked, and finally burned.[1] Rather than returning to the city after the destruction, the population seems to have dispersed and the site was abandoned. Ugarit passed out of memory, remaining buried until its rediscovery in 1929.

Ugarit was not alone in its fate. This period roughly between 1220 and 1150 BCE is often referred to as the Late Bronze Age Collapse. These years saw the destruction of the Mycenaean and Minoan kingdoms in Greece, the cities of Mesopotamia, the Hittite Empire in Anatolia, as well as cities in the Levant and Canaan. Cities were burned, trade was disrupted and finally ceased, and human populations declined precipitously. What caused the Bronze Age Collapse is still hotly debated in scholarly circles, and one of the more contentious questions concerns the role that climate change may have played in causing the collapse.

What is indisputable is that, just prior to the destruction of Ugarit, the entire Mediterranean area was experiencing a severe famine.[1] Clay tablets, many of them letters found in Egypt, Ugarit, and Hattusa, all describe the famine, sometimes in rather desperate language. One letter from the king of the Hittites demands that the king of Ugarit furnish a ship and crew to transport 2,000 measures of grain from Ugarit to the Hittite port of Ura. Furthermore, the author of the letter repeats several times that this is a matter of life or death.[2] These written sources, however, don't mention the cause(s) of the famine. The first reference as to a possible cause of this Mediterranean-wide famine, curiously enough, comes from Aristotle in his *Meteorologica*. He attributes the demise of the Greek city Mycenae, which was sacked and abandoned at about the same time as Ugarit, to a change in climate. Aristotle writes:[3]

> *Places that formerly enjoyed a good climate deteriorate and grow dry. This has happened in Greece to the land about Argos and Mycenae. In the time of the Trojan War [which was fought near the end of the Bronze age in about 2050 BCE], Argos was marshy and able to support few inhabitants only, while Mycenae was good land and therefore the more famous. Now the opposite is the case, for Mycenae has become unproductive and completely dry, while the Argive land that was once marshy and unproductive is now under cultivation. What has happened in this small district may therefore be supposed to happen to large districts and whole countries.*

In other words, Aristotle asserts that climate change contributed to a loss of agricultural productivity at Mycenae, which could explain why the city was not reoccupied after its destruction. Conversely, climate change also seems to have improved agricultural conditions in Argos.

In addition to climate changes, several other possible causes for the Late Bronze Age Collapse have been offered over the years. Prior to the 1960s, it was thought that invasions by people/barbarians, collectively referred to as the "Sea Peoples," caused the collapse. In 1966, however, Rhys Carpenter, like Aristotle before him, suggested that the decline of Mycenae could have been the result of climate change.[4] That suggestion was taken up in the 1960s by David Donley, a Ph.D. student at the University of Wisconsin. Donley analyzed rainfall records of a spatial drought that occurred in January of 1955 (when most precipitation in the Middle East occurs) and argued that a long-term occurrence of such a pattern could have driven the late Bronze Age population migrations within Greece.[5] In 1982 Barry Weiss, a mathematician working for Bell Laboratories, used a larger data set drawn from Greek, Turkish, Cypriot, and Syrian weather stations for the period 1951-1976. Using some very advanced mathematics, he analyzed the data and hypothesized that a drought-induced migration of peoples from Western Anatolia occurred in the twelfth century BCE.[6] He further hypothesized that the migrations were in some way associated with the movements of the mysterious Sea Peoples that systematically attacked and destroyed cities like Troy, Mycenae, and Ugarit.

These approaches, while certainly intriguing, did not provide any direct evidence of drought conditions at the end of the thirteenth century BCE in the Middle East. The first attempt at providing actual physical evidence was offered by David Kaniewski of the Universetè de Toulouse and colleagues in 2010.[7] Located on the Mediterranean coast thirty kilometers south of Ugarit, the Bronze Age city of Gibala was situated next to the modern Rumailiah River. Over the millennia, the river eroded into the limestone bedrock and deposited alluvial sediments that date from the Late Bronze Age (~1,200 BCE) through the Iron Age (~500 BCE). The research team retrieved two sediment cores, dated the sediments with carbon-14, and analyzed the sediments for the kinds of pollen that had been deposited (Figure 7.1).

The study's results indicated the presence of a fire-ash deposit at the end of the Bronze Age that correlated with the first destruction of Gibala and Ugarit. Prior to the destruction, the kinds of pollen species indicated a relatively moist climate. But after the destruction, the pollen abruptly changed to species characteristic of drier conditions at or near the collapse. Furthermore, the percentage of cultivated pollen species (~6%) and cereal grasses (~4%) were relatively high prior to and decreased immediately after the collapse (Fig. 7.1). Overall, the results suggest the onset of drought conditions at or near the collapse (~1,200 BCE) that lasted on and off for the next 350 years.

In another study published in 2012, Brandon Drake of the University

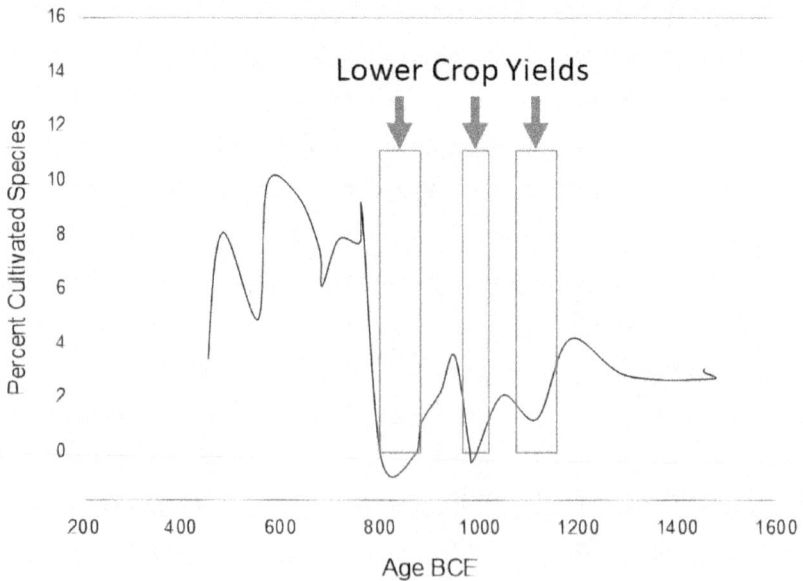

Figure 7.1. The Late Bronze Age collapse from the viewpoint of food availability. Figure shows the percent cultivated pollen species with the lower crop yields highlighted in red. Data is from Kaniewski et al., 2010[7].

of New Mexico used oxygen isotope data collected from speleothems (groundwater-precipitated limestones in caves) in Israel, stable carbon isotopes, alkenone-derived sea surface temperatures (SSTs), and changes in warm-species dinocysts and foraminifera in the Mediterranean Sea to detect possible climate changes over the last 3,000 years. Calcium carbonate ($CaCO_3$) speleothems (the stalactites and stalagmites that form in limestone caves) provide a record of the $^{18}O/^{16}O$ composition, and thus the temperature, of the groundwater from which the calcium carbonate precipitated over time. In addition, the stable carbon isotopic composition of plant material provides a record of the aridity of the climate the plants grew in. Sea surface temperatures give an indication of overall climatic temperatures, as do the relative abundance of warm-water dinocysts and foraminifera. Drake's results show a drop in precipitation near the time of the collapse, a drop in the $\delta^{13}C$ of pollen recovered from cores of Lake Voulkaria in western Greece indicating increased aridity, and a sharp drop in occupation of cities in Greece and Crete at the end of the Bronze age.[8] His results are consistent with a prolonged drought coinciding with the Late Bronze Age collapse (Figure 7.2).

Another method of determining the amount of rainfall falling on what is now Israel is by documenting the rise and fall of water levels in the Dead Sea over time. Because different water levels leave terraces showing where the lakeshore stood in the past, and because there is datable organic carbon in those sediments, it is possible to reconstruct the amount of rainfall at particular times in the past. Figure 7.3 shows the reconstructed precipitation over the last 4,000 years.[9] Note that the precipitation deduced from speleothem oxygen isotopes and carbon 13 (Fig. 7.2) substantially agrees with the estimates made from the Dead Sea water levels (Fig. 7.3). The agreement between these different indicators of drier or wetter conditions in the past (Figs. 7.1, 7.2, 7.3) considerably supports the notion that climate change could have been one factor leading to the Late Bronze Age collapse.

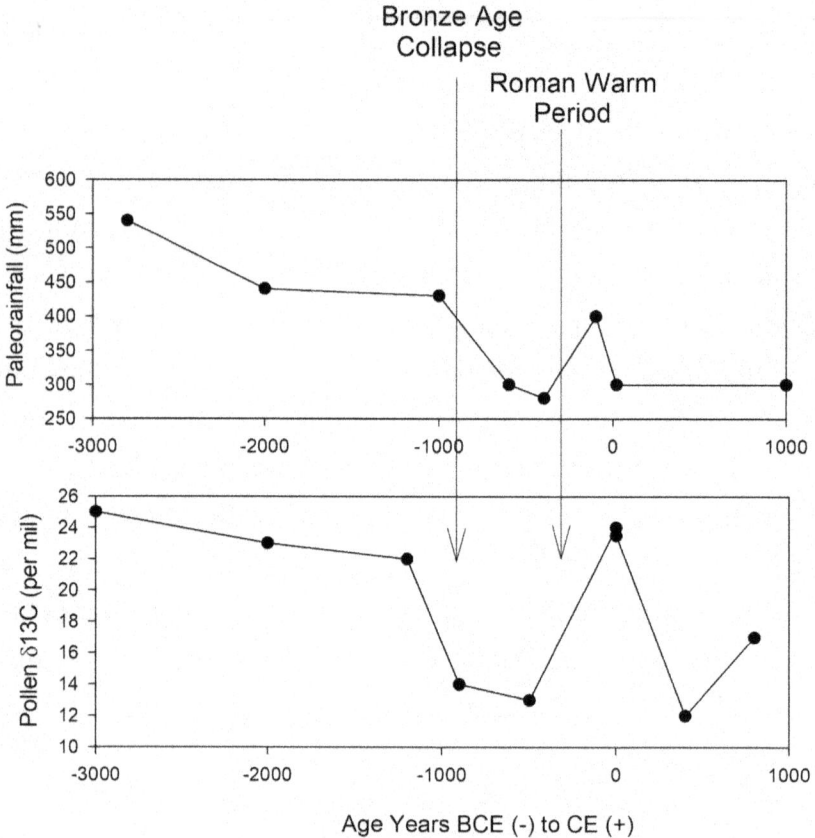

Figure 7.2. (A) Paleo annual rainfall reconstructed from oxygen-isotope speleothem data, and (B) ô13C discrimination calculated from pollen radiocarbon dates. Both records indicate a drop in precipitation beginning near the late Bronze Age collapse and continuing through the "Greek Dark Ages." Both records also indicate a climatic recovery during the Roman Warm Period. Data is from Drake, 2012.

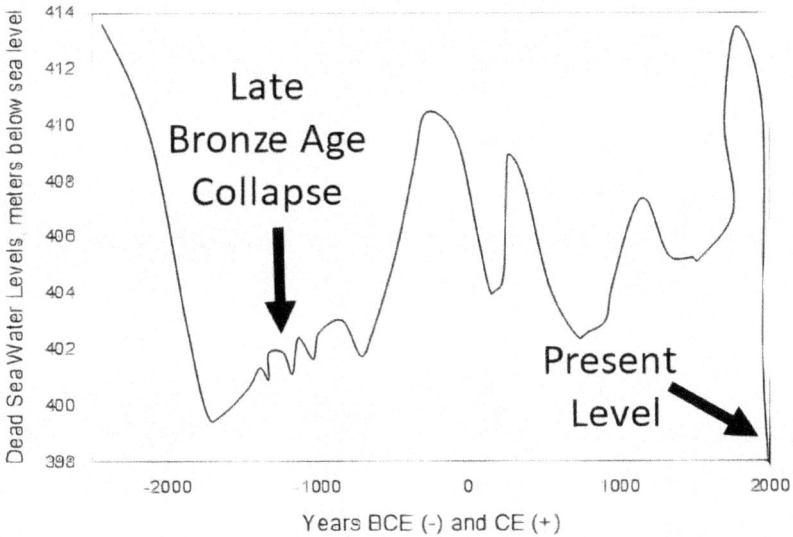

Fig. 7.3. A high-resolution water-level curve for the Dead Sea over the past 4000 years. Data is from Enzel et al., 2003[9].

But not everyone agrees with that conclusion. In 2016, Bernard Knapp of Glasgow University and Sturt Manning of Cornell University published a critique of Kaniewski's and Drake's conclusion that climate change was a principal factor that drove the Late Bronze Age collapse.[10] Knapp and Manning argued that "human societies of all kinds and in many different types of environments have shown their resilience to both long- and short-term episodes of climate change." Rather, they continued, "collapse results from multiple, cascading stress factors—politic-economic, demographic, and sociocultural as well as environmental—and the interrelationships among them." They also pointed out that the margin of error inherent in the carbon-14 dates used by Kaniewski and Drake were suspect, writing, "This is loose dating—within one or two centuries at best, and hardly the basis for a refined historical reconstruction."

Aside from the criticism of the carbon-14 dating, Knapp and Manning have a point that a lot more than climate change happened at the end of the Bronze Age. In 2011, Issam Halayqa of Birzeit University cataloged some of the issues that Ugarit was facing leading up to its destruction.[11] As Knapp and Manning would have expected, it was a typically human tangle. Because Ugarit was subordinate to the Hittite Empire, the Hittites demanded various tributes from the city. Because of the ongoing famine, some of that tribute would have been in the form of food shipments. In one letter, the Hittite king Šuppiluliuma II ordered "his servant," perhaps the king of Ugarit or one of the king's officials, to send food to the Hittites. Such demands would have been a significant economic burden and certainly would not have been welcome in Ugarit. In another letter, Ammurapi, the last king of Ugarit, denied having food to send, claiming there was a shortage of grain in Ugarit as well. While it may have been simply an excuse, it demonstrates that there was a certain amount of tension between Ugarit and the Hittites.

One political consequence of that tension was that king Ammurapi seems to have attempted to forge a political alliance with Egypt by requesting he be allowed to erect a statue of the Pharaoh Merneeptah in Ugarit's temple of Baal. The Egyptians, however, were having none of that. Egypt was the breadbasket of much of the Middle East, and the Hittites were certainly one of their best customers. There's not much to gain by irritating your customers. Unsurprisingly, Pharaoh rejected the request. That Ammurapi would have made such a gesture to Egypt would probably not have pleased the Hittites either. The net effect was more political tension between Ugarit, Egypt, and the Hittites.

Another source of political tension was that Ammurapi divorced his wife, a Hittite princess. The whole point of marriage at that time was to cement mutually advantageous political and military alliances, so Ammurapi's divorce would have weakened the alliance with the Hittites. Ammurapi further irritated the Hittites by not sending sufficient troops and warships to fulfill his military obligations, and those he did send were of such poor quality that they were of little use. To make matters worse, sending troops and ships to help the Hittites left Ugarit vulnerable to attack. When the seven ships attacked Ugarit, the city was ill prepared to resist and was subsequently sacked. It's plain that the city's demise stemmed from more than a changing climate.

Regardless, a drying climatic trend around 1,200 BCE almost certainly caused decreased agricultural production.[7,8] Such a decrease could easily explain the famine described in the Ugaritic texts, but there was a more subtle effect of climate change in the centuries leading up to the Bronze Age Collapse. That effect would be the warming trend, and higher amounts of precipitation in the years between 1,600 and 1,200 BCE that is indicated by carbon-13 trends in plant material (Fig. 7.1), carbon-13 trends in cave speleothems (Fig. 7.2), and water levels of the Dead Sea (Fig. 7.3). The warmer and wetter climate characteristic of the Middle Bronze Age would have encouraged grain cultivation and increased the available food supply. The inevitable consequence was an increase in population, a population that couldn't be sustained when the climate reversal led to cooler and drier conditions, explaining the onset of famine by 1,200 BCE. But more importantly, that pattern of an increasing human population during a warmer, wetter climate followed by famine as the climate cooled was to be repeated again and again in human history. The next episodes would be before, during, and after the Roman Warm Period (300 BCE to 400 CE), as well as before, during, and after the Medieval Warm Period (750 to 1300 CE).

REFERENCES

1. Astour, M.C., 1965. New evidence on the last days of Ugarit. American Journal of Archaeology, 69(3), pp.253-258.

2. Halayqa, I. and Yonge, C.M., 2011. The Demise of Ugarit in the Light of its Connections with Ḫatti. https://fada.birzeit.edu/handle/20.500.11889/4717.

3. Neumann, J., 1985. Climatic change as a topic in the classical Greek and Roman literature. Climatic Change, 7(4), pp.441-454.

4. Carpenter, R., 1966. Discontinuity in Greek Civilization. Cambridge University Press, Cambridge, 88 pp.

5. Bryson, R.A., Lamb, H.H. and Donley, D.L., 1974. Drought and the decline of Mycenae. Antiquity, 48(189), pp.46-50.

6. Weiss, B., 1982. The decline of Late Bronze Age civilization as a possible response to climatic change. Climatic Change, 4(2), pp.173-198.

7. Kaniewski, D., Paulissen, E., Van Campo, E., Weiss, H., Otto, T., Bretschneider, J. and Van Lerberghe, K., 2010. Late second–early first millennium BC abrupt climate changes in coastal Syria and their possible significance for the history of the Eastern Mediterranean. Quaternary Research, 74(2), pp.207-215.

8. Drake, B.L., 2012. The influence of climatic change on the Late Bronze Age Collapse and the Greek Dark Ages. Journal of Archaeological Science, 39(6), pp.1862-1870.

9. Enzel, Y., Bookman, R., Sharon, D., Gvirtzman, H., Dayan, U., Ziv, B. and Stein, M., 2003. Late Holocene climates of the Near East deduced from Dead Sea level variations and modern regional winter rainfall. Quaternary Research, 60(3), pp.263-273.

10. Knapp, A.B. and Manning, S.W., 2016. Crisis in context: The ende of the Late Bronze Age in the eastern Mediterranean. American Journal of Archaeology, 120(1), pp. 99-149.

11. Halayqa, I.K., Dietrich, M. and Loretz, O., 2010. The demise of Ugarit in the light of its connections with Ḫatti. Ugarit-Forschungen, 42, pp. 297-330.

CHAPTER 8
Warming and Cooling: The Rise and Fall of Rome

THE BEGINNING OF THE MIGHTY Roman Empire, curiously enough, had its roots in one of Rome's greatest military defeats. In either 390 or 387 BCE, a tribe of Celts called the Senones living in northern Italy attacked and defeated the Roman army at the Battle of the Allia just outside of Rome. Apparently the Senones were irritated that Rome had reneged on a diplomatic treaty. These fair-skinned Celtic warriors with blonde or reddish hair were typically taller and more heavily muscled than the Romans. They also fought with a fury that apparently unnerved the Romans. Wielding long double-edged iron swords, the Celts attacked, breaking the Roman formations and sending the survivors fleeing to Rome. A few days later, the Senones sacked Rome, staying for seven months. They finally agreed to leave if the Romans paid a ransom of 1,000 pounds of gold. According to the Roman historian Livy, a Tribune complained that the scales used to weigh the gold were rigged. Thereupon which the Senones' leader threw his sword and scabbard onto the scale's counterweight increasing the ransom and shouted "Vae Victis" or "woe to the vanquished."

This ignominious defeat and the shame of having agreed to pay a ransom (it's not clear if they actually paid) shocked the Romans to their core. They elected a general named Marcus Furius Camillus dictator for a year so he could confront the Celts. Camillus defeated the Senones at the battle of Tusculum soon after the Battle of the Allia, but the damage to the Roman psyche was done. They rebuilt their city, adding a wall for protection against the Celts. They also seem to have changed the infantry tactics they used to fight the Celts. Realizing that the average Roman soldier could not match the physical strength of the average Celt, they developed a highly sophisticated system of infantry formations and maneuvers designed to protect themselves behind a shield wall. Rather than using long slashing swords like the Celts, they used short stabbing swords and spears that were better suited for the close fighting behind a shield wall. These tactics required a lot of practice, and the Roman legions of the next several hundred years became famous for their rigorous training and tactical skill. Fighting cooperatively rather than as individuals (as the Celts did) often gave the Romans a decisive edge in battle, particularly when fighting undisciplined barbarians. The Romans then proceeded to systematically conquer most of Italy, mainly to keep their neighbors from trying to conquer them.

From a climate point of view, however, the date of the Battle of the Allia (390 or 387 BCE) is notable because it was fought when Europe was experiencing a pronounced dip in its average temperatures (Figure 8.1). Average temperatures in Europe over the past 10,000 years have been estimated with a number of proxy indicators including Total Solar Irradiance (TSI) estimated from ^{14}C present in tree rings, $\delta^{18}O$ from ice cores, $\delta^{18}O$ from speleothems (carbonates in cave stalactites and stalagmites), and lake varves.[1] The data set in Fig. 8.1 estimates temperature changes in Europe using thousands of ^{14}C measurements in tree rings, and indicates a substantial temperature dip in 390 BCE.[2] It's possible that had something to do with restlessness of the Senones, but we'll never know. What we do know is that by 300 BCE, temperatures had recovered, ushering in what has variously been termed the "Roman Warm Period" or alternatively the "Roman Climate Optimum," that lasted until roughly 400 CE (Fig. 8.1)[3].

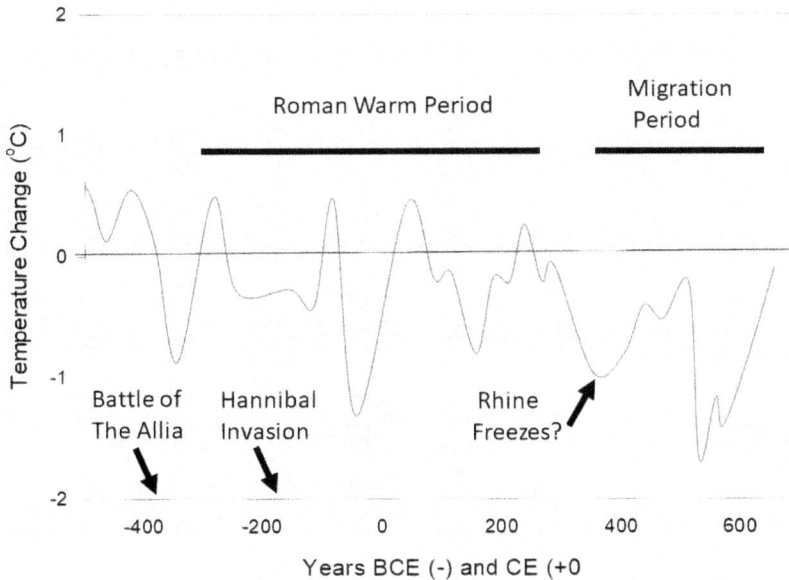

Figure 8.1. Temperature anomalies in central Europe deduced from ^{14}C of tree rings. Data is from Büntgen et al., 2011.[2]

The Roman Warm Period coincided with the height of the Roman Republic and the beginning of the Roman Empire, a fact that some climate-oriented historians do not think is a coincidence.[3] The chief characteristic of the Roman Warm Period was unusual climate stability. Not only was the weather warmer than it had been in the past, but it was also wetter. Ptolemy of Alexandria (ca. 100-170 CE), the leading Roman scientist of his day, reported that it rained in Alexandria every month except August.[4] As an astronomer who carefully studied the night sky, Ptolemy was uniquely qualified to report knowledgably when it did and did not rain. Ptolemy conveys that his weather was certainly wetter than Alexandria is today (when rain is practically non-existent between June and September). The combination of a warm, wet, and relatively stable climate enabled better and more consistent harvests, meaning that the population of Italy, most of which was under Roman control at the beginning of the Punic Wars (264 to 146 BCE), could grow. In retrospect, its enormous population (by ancient stan-dards) would become one of Rome's greatest military assets in fighting and eventually winning the Punic wars against the Carthaginians.

The first of the three Punic Wars between Rome and Carthage began in 264 BCE and was largely fought over possession of Sicily. At first, Rome was at a decided disadvantage because it didn't have a navy whereas the Carthaginians, descended from the Phoenicians, were expert seamen. With characteristic doggedness, the Romans built a fleet, and after twenty-three years of incessant but inconclusive fight-ing, Rome forced Carthage to sue for peace. Rome took possession of Sicily, Carthage was made to pay a large indemnity, but the strategic competition between the two empires remained unresolved, leading to the second Punic War (218 to 201 BCE).

The second Punic War began when Hannibal, a Carthaginian general, invaded Spain and captured the city of Saguntum. Because Saguntum was a Roman ally, Rome declared war on Carthage in 218 BCE. With winter approaching, Hannibal did something that took the Romans totally by surprise. Rather than going into camp for the winter, Hannibal marched his army of 50,000 infantry and 9,000 cav-alry over the Pyrenees Mountains into what is now France. When he reached the Rhône River, a considerable barrier, the opposite bank was defended by an army of Celts allied with Rome. Borrowing a tactic from Alexander the Great, Hannibal divided his army and secretly sent a contingent north to cross the river twenty-five miles upstream. The plan was for Hannibal to spend several days assembling boats and rafts for a crossing, noisily making sure the Celts' attention was focused on him. Meanwhile, the second contingent would quietly approach the Celts from the north to surprise them. When everything was in place, Hannibal himself led the crossing. As the Celts surged forward to meet Hannibal's boats, the second Carthaginian contingent made a surprise attack on their exposed flank. The Celts immediately fled, and the battle was over in minutes.

The river crossed, the way was now open to cross the Alps and attack Rome directly. The problem, however, was that it was now November and crossing the Alps in the winter would be difficult enough for individual travelers but would be nearly impossible for an entire army. In 218 BCE, the weather was firmly in the Roman Warm Period, with temperatures possibly higher than they are today (Fig. 8.1). That warmth may well have been a factor in Hannibal's successful crossing. Although the weather was certainly cold and snowy in the Alps, the army does seem to have been spared debilitating blizzards that might have stopped them altogether. After Hannibal's army crossed the pass to the Italian side (scholars still argue over the exact pass), the going became more difficult. The ground would freeze during the night, of course, but during the day, the southward-facing ground would melt, making the narrow tract a slippery nightmare. The footing for both men and packhorses became treacherous, and not a few of them slipped and fell to their deaths.

By the time Hannibal crossed the Alps, he probably had lost about half of his army. But northern Italy was still the home of several Celtic tribes who had been badly treated by Rome ever since the Battle of the Allia. The Celts flocked to Hannibal's army, thinking they could get back at the hated Romans. Hannibal, for his part, made very good use of these new troops. Thinking it best to strike at Hannibal while his army was still depleted, the Romans sent an army north under the command of Sempronius Longus. The two armies met on the plain of the River Trebia. After a few days of skirmishing, which convinced Sempronius that he had the upper hand, battle commenced on December 22 or 23, 218 BCE. The Romans had about 42,000 men, Hannibal had about 30,000, and Sempronius' strategy was to simply overwhelm the Carthaginians by strength of numbers. But Hannibal, as he had done during the crossing of the Rhône River, secretly sent a contingent of cavalry behind the Romans and had them hide from view. He next lured the Romans out of their camp by sending his light cavalry to harass the Roman pickets and provoke a fight. When the Roman cavalry responded, they were ambushed by the heavy Carthaginian cavalry. Simultaneously, the Carthaginian cavalry that Hannibal had sent behind the Romans struck the Roman formation in the rear. This routed the Romans, giving Hannibal a decisive victory.

The Battle of the Trebia set the pattern for much of the rest of Hannibal's Italian campaign. Hannibal was usually outnumbered, but by deft maneuvering and all-around good generalship, he won battle after battle. In the spring of 217 BCE, Hannibal ambushed a Roman army at the Battle of Lake Trasimene and killed as many as 15,000 Romans. The next year the Romans attacked the Carthaginians at Cannae, but Hannibal used a double envelopment maneuver to surround the Romans. Once they had the Romans surrounded, the Carthaginians systematically hacked all of them to death. Incredibly, the Roman historian Livy writing in the first century BCE, reported that 50,000 Romans were killed. Cannae was a disaster of unbelievable proportions for the Romans, the worst defeat they had ever suffered.

Amazingly, the Romans managed to come back again and again. They did this by expanding the age and physical standards for new soldiers and by allowing convicted criminals to serve as well. None of those adjustments would have been possible without the increase in Rome's population over the last hundred years that at least partly resulted from the Roman Warm Period. In the end, Rome won the Second Punic War out of sheer weight of numbers as well as a stubborn refusal to admit that they could be beaten. Hannibal, certainly the finest general in the ancient world on par with Alexander, simply couldn't overcome Rome's overwhelming manpower advantage. Eventually, the Romans decided the only way to finally beat the Carthaginians was to stop pursuing Hannibal in Italy and take the war directly to Africa.

To that end, Publius Cornelius Scipio invaded the Carthaginian homeland in 204 BCE, defeating the Carthaginians in two major battles and winning the allegiance of the Numidian kingdoms of North Africa. Hannibal and the remnants of his army in Italy were recalled to Carthage, but it was too little, too late. Scipio, unlike many of the Roman Generals at the time, was a fine tactician. He finally managed to engage and defeat Hannibal at the Battle of Zama (near modern Zama, Tunisia) in 202 BCE. This victory earned Scipio the title Scipio Africanus, the name by which he is known today. Now out of options, the Carthaginians had to sue for peace. The Second Punic War was over. Fifty years later, Rome embarked on a Third Punic War which ended with the total destruction of Carthage in 146 BCE.

The population increase that began with the onset of the Roman Warm Period (~300 BCE) was, given the challenges of Hannibal's invasion of Italy, a good thing for Rome. Without it, Rome wouldn't have had the manpower to outlast and eventually overwhelm Hannibal's tactical superiority. Rome's population increase continued after the establishment of the Empire in 44 BCE. It is estimated that Italy's population increased from ten million the year Augustus died (14 CE) to fourteen million in 165 CE, an increase of 29%[3].

But population increases can also have a downside, especially in the ancient world. Being in possession of Egypt and its vast agricultural resources, Rome was largely buffered from famine, but it wasn't buffered from infectious diseases inevitable with such a large and dense population. In the winter of 165 CE, the Roman army was besieging the Mesopotamian city of Seleucia when a plague, probably smallpox, broke out. The Antonine Plague, as it is known, raged from 165 to 180

CE, quickly spreading throughout the whole empire. It is estimated that the plague killed between five and ten million people at a time when the entire empire's population was about seventy-five million.[3] The Roman legions were affected disproportionally, and it caused a severe manpower shortage. The Roman Warm Period, and the subsequent increase in population, turned out to have been a crucial factor in Rome's rise to dominance in the Mediterranean world. Conversely, the increased population almost certainly contributed to increased incidence of disease, of which the Antonine Plague is just one example.

The Roman Warm Period was not destined to last forever. Beginning in the third century CE, the climate in Europe began to cool. The Roman population wasn't the only one to have grown during the Roman Warm Period. The population of the barbarian tribes living outside the Empire grew as well. The cooler weather caused food shortages and, just as had happened at the end of the Bronze Age, it caused what has been termed a Migration Period (Figure 8.1).

The winter of 406 CE was exceptionally cold along the Rhine River in what is now Germany. Wide, swift, and deep, the Rhine River had long served as a barrier, effectively keeping Germanic tribes from entering and attacking the Roman Province of Gaul. That winter, anywhere from 100,000 to 150,000 Germanic warriors and their families were camped on the eastern side of the river, hoping to cross into Gaul. Some historians say the Germanic tribes were fleeing after being attacked by the Huns invading from the east. Others say that the tribes were simply intent on plundering Gaul. Regardless of the tribes' motivation, the Rhine was still a formidable barrier that couldn't easily be breached. But the cold weather might have changed that. According to a contemporary chronicler named Prosper of Aquitaine, the tribes managed to cross the river en masse on December 31, 406 CE. Prosper doesn't say how the tribesmen accomplished that feat, but cross it they did. The suddenness of that crossing, and the cold winter weather led the eighteenth-century historian Edward Gibbon to speculate that the Rhine River had frozen solid, and the tribesmen simply walked across it:

> *The victorious confederates [i.e. the Germanic barbarians] pursued their march, and on the last day of the year, in a season when the waters of the Rhine were most probably frozen, they entered without opposition the defenseless provinces of Gaul. This memorable passage of the Suevi, the Vandals, the Alani, and the Burgundians, who never afterwards retreated, may be considered as the fall of the Roman Empire in the countries beyond the Alps.*

It's unusual for the Rhine River to freeze, but it does happen periodically. The last time such a freeze happened in the modern era was during the exceptionally cold winter of 1962-63. (I was living in Germany at the time, and I well remember how cold it was). However they crossed the Rhine, the tribesmen sacked Gaul. Many of the thoroughly Romanized Celts, including Prosper of Aquitaine, fled and became refugees. The Germanic tribes eventually reached Rome in 410 CE, which they sacked, marking the beginning of the end of the Western Roman Empire.

The last six hundred years of the Roman Empire in the west has a climate history that in many ways mirrors what happened during the Bronze Age (Chapter 7). The Middle Bronze Age was characterized by a warm and relatively wet climate favorable for agricultural production leading to a population increase. When the climate turned drier near the end of the Bronze Age, those populations could not be sustained, causing famine. Famine was certainly one factor that led to the end-of-the Bronze Age migration of peoples and their assault on the civilizations of Mesopotamia, the Hittites, Mycenae, and Egypt.

Like the Middle Bronze Age, the Roman Warm Period fostered an increasing population. Unlike the Bronze Age, that did not lead to widespread famine in Italy, largely because Rome controlled the vast agricultural production of Egypt. However, the larger population does seem to have been a factor in the spread of infectious diseases such as the Antonine Plague. Finally, like the end of the Bronze Age, the subsequent cooling trend after 400 CE was one factor contributing to the migration of Germanic peoples into the Empire. Those migrations, like those at the end of the Bronze Age, led to a total societal collapse in the Western Roman Empire.

That pattern—population growth during a relatively warm period followed by agricultural stress, famine, and disease when the climate reversed and became cooler—was about to be repeated in Europe during the Middle Ages.

REFERENCES

1. McCormick, M., Büntgen, U., Cane, M.A., Cook, E.R., Harper, K., Huybers, P., Litt, T., Manning, S.W., Mayewski, P.A., More, A.F. and Nicolussi, K., 2012. Climate change during and after the Roman Empire: reconstructing the past from scientific and historical evidence. Journal of Interdisciplinary History, 43(2), pp.169-220.

2. Büntgen, U., Tegel, W., Nicolussi, K., McCormick, M., Frank, D., Trouet, V., Kaplan, J.O., Herzig, F., Heussner, K.U., Wanner, H. and Luterbacher, J., 2011. 2500 years of European climate variability and human susceptibility. Science, 331(6017), pp.578-582.

3. Harper, K., 2017. The fate of Rome. Princeton University Press. Princeton and Oxford, 415 pp.

4. Lehoux, D. 2007. Astronomy, weather, and calendars in the ancient world: Parapegmata and Related Texts in Classical and Near-Eastern Societies: Cambridge University Press, Cambridge/New York 566 pp.

CHAPTER 9
Cooling, Warming and the Viking Age of Expansion

THE ROMAN WARM PERIOD (~300 BCE to 400 CE) was not only good news for the Roman Empire; it was also very good news for the "barbarians" living in northern Europe. An investigation of farming practices in what is now Sweden shows a significant expansion of land under cultivation beginning about 200 BCE.[1] The archeological evidence for this includes the stone-wall complexes that were established during that period and used to enclose fields, probably for raising cattle. These complexes were associated with the foundations of large rectangular halls that were used communally by extended families numbering from twenty to thirty individuals. In addition, the kinds of pollen recovered from dated sediments indicate a transition from closed forests to more open fields.

But just like what happened to the Western Roman Empire, the onset of a cooling trend around 400 CE had disastrous consequences in Scandinavia. Contributing to that cooling trend may have been a decrease in solar radiation reaching the earth, as reconstructed by variations in ^{14}C production in the upper atmosphere. Beginning almost exactly in 400 CE, the Total Solar Irradiance (TSI) reaching the earth turned sharply lower, reaching a minimum about 450 CE (Figure 9.1).[2] Just what may have caused this sudden drop in TSI in 400 CE is not particularly clear. In any case, a drop in solar radiation, particularly in northern latitudes, would necessarily result in decreased agricultural production.

TSI Drop At the end of the Roman Warm Period

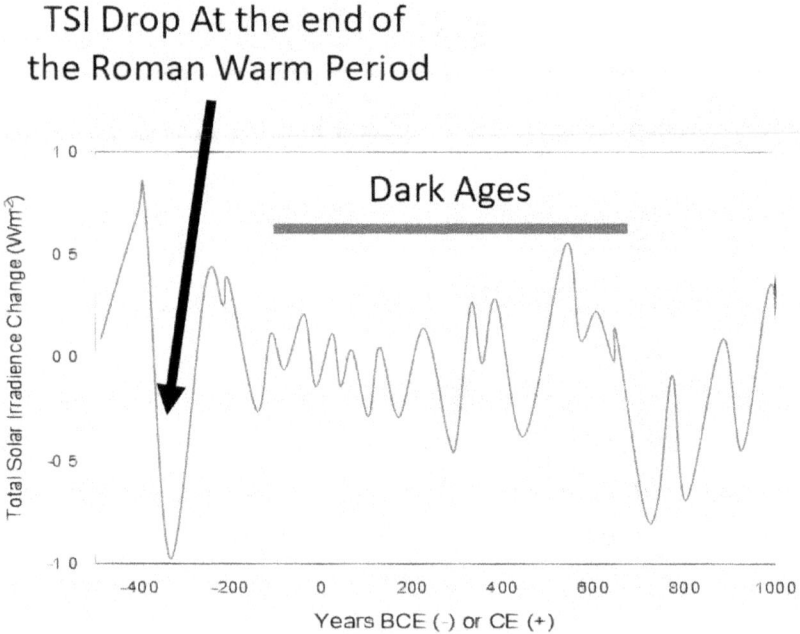

Figure 9.1. Changes in solar activity (Total Solar Irradiance (TSI)) as indicated by changes in atmospheric ^{14}C production. Data from McCormick et al[2].

By 400 CE, the population in Scandinavia was probably approaching the carrying capacity of the available farmland anyway. That being the case, the natural consequence of any lowering of crop production would be a famine. Presumably, the cooling trend that began in 400 CE would have begun to moderate after 450 CE as TSI rebounded. That moderation may have actually happened between 450 and 500 CE, but then an unknown climate stressor entered the picture. In 536 CE, a large volcanic eruption occurred somewhere in the northern latitudes that injected huge amounts of sulfur aerosols into the atmosphere.[3] That eruption certainly would have had at least a temporary cooling effect planet-wide, but Mother Nature wasn't quite done yet. In 539 CE, a volcano now known as Ilopango located in modern El Salvador also exploded violently.[4] Incredibly, it is estimated that as much as 43 cubic kilometers (km³) of ash, along with large amounts of sulfur aerosols, was blown into the atmosphere. (By way of comparison, the 1980 eruption of Mount St. Helens in Washington State produced only 4.2 km³ of ash.) But again, Mother Nature was still not done. A few years after that, in 547 CE another smaller, but still significant, volcanic eruption occurred.

The ash and sulfur aerosols from a single volcanic eruption can disrupt the warming effects of solar radiation, but the effects are typically fairly transient, dispersing in two or three years.[5] When three or more large eruptions happen within the space of a decade, other atmospheric or oceanic processes can amplify the cooling effects. Specifically, sudden atmospheric cooling by volcanism can trigger feedback loops that accelerate the overall cooling trend. One feedback might be a sustained weakening of northward heat transport by ocean currents. Another possibility is that short-term temperature drops cause rapid expansion of sea ice at high latitudes. That expansion, in turn, could increase the amount of solar radiation being reflected into space, causing further cooling. In any case, the cooling trend that began in 537 CE lasted for several centuries and has come to be called the Late Antique Little Ice Age, or LALIA.

The overall effect of the LALIA was a sharp decrease in summertime temperatures, not just in Scandinavia, but around the world. As we've seen before, such climate reversals can result in crop failures, famine, epidemics, and political instability. Between 541 and 543 CE, for example, widespread food shortages in the Eastern Roman Empire were followed by a devastating epidemic of bubonic plague. In China, the Northern Wei Dynasty collapsed (~540 CE). In the Steppes of Mongolia, the dominant Rouran tribes were displaced by the Eastern Turks (~551 CE). At about the same time, the Avars arrived north of the Black Sea and came into conflict with the Byzantines (~550 CE). The Persian Empire was attacked by the Western Turks (~625 CE), contributing to its later collapse in the face of the Arabian Islamic Empire. There's simply no doubt that the LALIA was a contributing factor to these disruptive historical events.

Cassiodorus (485-585 CE), a Roman administrator in the service of Theodoric the Great, king of the Ostrogoths, gave a vivid description of the strange weather experienced in Italy following the initiation of the LALIA:

> *The sun, first of stars, seems to have lost his wonted light and appears of a bluish color. We marvel to see no shadows of our bodies at noon, to feel the mighty vigor of his heat wasted into feebleness, and the phenomena that accompany a transitory eclipse prolonged through a whole year.*
>
> *The moon, too, even when her orb is full, is empty of her natural splendor. Strange has been the course of the year thus far. We have had a winter without storms, a spring without mildness, and a summer without heat. Whence can we look for harvest, since the months which should have been maturing the corn have been chilled by Boreas?*

Unsurprisingly, famine ensued in Italy.

In Scandinavia, the period between 400 and 600 CE is notable for the abandonment of farms and the paucity of rich burials.[1] It has been estimated that as many 15%-20% of the farms that had been active prior to 400 CE were abandoned and the population seems to have decreased by a factor of two.[6] How much starvation contributed to that decrease in population is impossible to say. No doubt some people simply left Scandinavia in the hopes of finding more productive land elsewhere. If they did, they would have been joining the many other peoples and tribes restlessly moving around much of the world in what has been termed the "Migration Period" (~400-600 CE).

Interestingly, the idea of long, cold, dark winters, such as those which had followed the eruption of Ilopango, may have formed a cultural memory in the oral traditions of Scandinavia. The Icelandic historian and poet Snorri Sturluson (1179-1241 CE) records in his Prose Edda:

First of all that a winter will come called Fimbulwinter.
Then snow will drift from all directions.
There will then be great frosts and keen winds.
The sun will do no good.
There will be three of these winters together
And no summer between.

The description of the Fimbulwinter by Snorri, written down more than 500 years after the Ilopango eruption, is eerily similar to Cassiodorus' contemporary description given above. Could Fimbulwinter be a Scandinavian cultural memory of the years following 539 CE and the LALIA?

The previous Roman Warm Period had seen a steady increase in land under cultivation in Europe, significant tree-cutting activity, and an increase in open meadowland. In sediments of the middle Lahn Valley in what is now Germany, the Roman Warm Period was characterized by an increase in riverine sedimentation due to soil erosion (farming), a decrease in oak logs deposited with riverine sediments, and a decrease in pollen from oak trees (lumber harvesting), and an increase in pollen associated with open meadowland.[7]

During the Migration Period following the beginning of the LALIA, there was a decrease in riverine sedimentation, an increase in oak logs deposited with river sediments, and a decrease in pollen associated with meadowlands. All of this indicates a marked decrease in human agricultural activity[7] as had also been observed in Scandinavia.[1] Not unexpectedly, many of the migrating Germanic peoples and tribes moved southwards towards modern Italy and Spain, suggesting that a colder climate was a factor driving those migrations.

After 700 CE, however, solar irradiance rebounded again (Fig. 9.1), initiating a warming trend known as the Medieval Warm Period, which lasted from about 750 to 1300 CE. With the Migration Period largely over by 750 CE, and with a steadily warming climate in Europe, the population settled down and expanded again. This expansion was particularly pronounced in Scandinavia. Not only did the overall population increase, but the farming practices changed as well. In the earlier expansion period (200 BCE to 400 CE), the farms were characterized by enclosing stone walls and the foundations of large halls serving what were probably one or more extended families. After 600 CE, the trend was toward single-family farms with different families inhabiting small hamlets or villages.[1] As the population expanded, once again the amount of arable land in Scandinavia became a limiting factor, and once again some portion of that population was obliged to migrate.

It wasn't just the warming climate that contributed to an increasing population in Scandinavia, part of it was the conjugal customs that were being practiced. Specifically, the Danes, Swedes, and Norse practiced polygamy in which economically successful men had up to three or four wives.[6] That, in turn, meant a significant increase in the number of babies being born to these families. Furthermore, since the Scandinavians also practiced primogenitor (the oldest son inherited the farm), younger sons had to find some other means of making a living. One option was to go somewhere else. But leave and do what?

Given the extremely advanced ship-building and navigation technology the Scandinavians had developed, one answer was to find other places to build farms, initiating what is now called the Viking Age of Expansion. This era featured several expansion strategies. One strategy was internal expansion, in which a younger son left to start a farm somewhere nearby. Another strategy was external expansion, in which the younger sons left on ships to find new land outside of Scandinavia. In relatively short order, the Norse established settlements in such diverse places as the Hebrides Islands, the Orkney Islands, Iceland, and Greenland. Another strategy was using their ship and sailing technology to trade northern goods, such as walrus ivory and furs. Scandinavian traders ranged as far east as Byzantium and as far south as Sicily. But there were other less-peaceful applications of their sailing and navigation technology: raiding and plundering.

The Viking Age of Expansion came to Britain in 793 CE when, as the Anglo-Saxon Chronicle records:

> *In the same year, on 8 June, the ravages of heathen men*
> *miserably destroyed God's church on Lindisfarne, with*
> *plunder and slaughter.*

Those "heathen men" were primarily the younger sons of the burgeoning families of Scandinavia. Furthermore, these Scandinavian men were typically taller and heavier than men of the other Germanic tribes inhabiting Europe at that time. Climate probably had something to do with that difference as well. The rate that heat is lost from the human body depends on the ratio of body mass to its surface area. In humans, body mass (m) increases proportionally as to the *cube* of body height (h) as in $m \approx h^3$. The body's surface area (sa), on the other hand, is only proportional to the *square* of body height as in $sa \approx h^2$, and surface area is what controls the loss of heat from the body. In cold climates, therefore, there is a distinct advantage in being tall and massive ($m \approx h^3$) because the surface of the human body loses heat less rapidly ($sa \approx h^2$). Scandinavians in the eighth century, as well as Scandinavians of today, tend to be taller than other Europeans. Conversely, in hot climates such as Viet Nam there is a distinct advantage in being able to disperse heat more easily, and thus the people in warm climes tend to be shorter and less massive.

Given the warrior culture of the Scandinavians, their highly advanced ship-building and sailing technology, and their large body frames, one strategy was to go "viking." Note that "viking" is a verb, so to "go viking" was an activity, most broadly referring to a sea journey whose purpose was to make some sort of profit. The activity could encompass fishing, trading, or in some instances, piracy.

The Danish warriors who ravaged Lindisfarne in 793 CE had chosen the latter option. Their target was the gold and silver objects that they knew could be found in Christian churches. Because Lindisfarne was a famous destination for pilgrims, there would also be the silver coins the pilgrims brought to the monastery as sacred offerings. By the standards of the day, Lindisfarne was a very rich enterprise, so attacking and sacking it was a guaranteed profit. It was the beginning of the Viking Age of Violent Expansion.

In the late eighth and early ninth centuries, these Viking expeditions of the piratical sort were largely hit-and-run operations involving three or four ships manned by fewer than 150 warriors. In Britain and Ireland, these raids focused on churches and monasteries because of their gold and silver. Also, churches and monasteries were largely undefended, making them easy targets. The risk/reward ratio was clearly in favor of the Viking raiders. As time passed, however, the raids became larger and more organized. In the year 840 CE, for example, the Anglo-Saxon Chronicle records that Æthelwulf of Wessex was defeated at Carhampton, Somerset, after thirty-five Viking ships had landed in the area.

For the first fifty years of the Viking Violent Expansion, the raids occurred in the summer months with the Vikings taking their booty home to Scandinavia. This pattern changed after 865 CE. By this point, the Vikings were thoroughly familiar with much of Britain, Ireland,

and France, and they had observed the abundant rich farmlands. Furthermore, the population in Scandinavia continued to increase, partly fueled by the wealth the Vikings brought home. By 865 CE, another generation of younger sons looking for gainful employment had cast their hungry eyes on those farmlands abroad.

In 866 CE, a largely Danish army landed in Northumbria, England. It's been estimated the army had between 1,000 and 2,000 warriors and had arrived in a fleet consisting of up to a hundred ships. This was no small raid, and the army quickly captured the Saxon city of Eoferwic, a name which the Vikings couldn't pronounce and which they renamed Jorvik, or modern York. By 875 CE, the Vikings had captured or controlled most of the Saxon kingdoms of Northumbria, Mercia, and East Anglia. Wessex, the last kingdom standing, was attacked in 878 CE and, after some initial successes, the Vikings were decisively defeated by the Saxon King Alfred the Great at the battle of Edington.

Alfred's victory ushered in a long period of Saxon resurgence that included Alfred recapturing London (886 CE), his son Edward defeating a Danish army at the Battle of Tettenhall (910 CE) in Mercia, and his grandson Æthelstan defeating a coalition of Irish Norse, Strathclyde Norse, and Scots at the Battle of Brunanburh (937 CE). The period of Viking Expansion was winding down by the end of the tenth century, but the Scandinavians already in Britain were there to stay, just as they stayed in Ireland (Dublin), France (Normandy), Russia, and even Byzantium. None of that could have happened without the increasing Scandinavian population that accompanied the Medieval Warm Period.

It's fashionable these days to think of climate change in apocalyptic terms. The history of population growth during the Roman Warm Period, followed by the cooling trend that ushered in the agonies of the LALIA and the Migration Period, supports such a viewpoint. We can be fairly certain that when the Norse raiders arrived at Lindisfarne in

793 CE, none of the monks who survived would have had the slightest inkling that the conflagration might have been caused simply by an increasing Scandinavian population. They would have had even less of an inkling that the population increase was due to a warming climate that followed the end of the Migration Period.

But given our not-quite twenty-twenty retrospective, we can be pretty sure that that was indeed the case.

REFERENCES

1. Widgren, M., 1983. Settlement and farming systems in the early Iron Age: a study of fossil agrarian landscapes in Östergötland, Sweden (Doctoral dissertation, Almqvist & Wiksell international), Stockholm, Sweden, 138 pp.

2. McCormick, M., Büntgen, U., Cane, M.A., Cook, E.R., Harper, K., Huybers, P., Litt, T., Manning, S.W., Mayewski, P.A., More, A.F. and Nicolussi, K., 2012. Climate change during and after the Roman Empire: reconstructing the past from scientific and historical evidence. Journal of Interdisciplinary History, 43(2), pp.169-220.

3. Büntgen, U., Myglan, V.S., Ljungqvist, F.C., McCormick, M., Di Cosmo, N., Sigl, M., Jungclaus, J., Wagner, S., Krusic, P.J., Esper, J. and Kaplan, J.O., 2016. Cooling and societal change during the Late Antique Little Ice Age from 536 to around 660 AD. Nature geoscience, 9(3), pp.231-236.

4. Dull, R.A., Southon, J.R., Kutterolf, S., Anchukaitis, K.J., Freundt, A., Wahl, D.B., Sheets, P., Amaroli, P., Hernandez, W., Wiemann, M.C. and Oppenheimer, C., 2019. Radiocarbon and geologic evidence reveal Ilopango volcano as source of the colossal 'mystery' eruption of 539/40 CE. Quaternary Science Reviews, 222, p.105855.

5. Hegerl, G.C., Crowley, T.J., Baum, S.K., Kim, K.Y. and Hyde, W.T., 2003. Detection of volcanic, solar and greenhouse gas signals in paleo-reconstructions of Northern Hemispheric temperature. Geophysical Research Letters, 30(5).

6. Sharpe, J.C., 2002. The Viking expansion: Climate, population, plunder.

Master's Thesis, University of Montana, 57 pp.

7. Zolitschka, B., Behre, K.E. and Schneider, J., 2003. Human and climatic impact on the environment as derived from colluvial, fluvial and lacustrine archives—examples from the Bronze Age to the Migration Period, Germany. Quaternary Science Reviews, 22(1), pp.81-100

CHAPTER 10
The High Middle Ages Climate Reversal and The Little Ice Age

THE WINTER OF 1191 CE was not the most auspicious time to be crossing the Alps, but Eleanor of Aquitaine was determined to make the trip. Her son Richard the Lionheart, the new King of England, was already in Sicily organizing what would become the Third Crusade. But before he could leave to go to the Holy Land, he had to secure the southern border of his lands in France. To that end, he had negotiated a dynastic marriage with the King of Navarre's daughter, Berengaria. The problem was, Richard was in Sicily and Berengaria was still in Navarre. For the marriage to happen, which according to the marriage contract had to be before Richard reached the Holy Land, Berengaria would have to come to Sicily. Eleanor of Aquitaine, even though she was sixty-nine years old, took on the job of escorting the bride-to-be over the Alps. In the Middle Ages, the church did not allow people to marry during the season of Lent, and so it was crucial they reach Sicily before February 27 when Lent began. That meant they had to make their crossing in the dead of winter.

Fortunately for Eleanor and Berengaria, Europe's climate was in the midst of the Medieval Warm Period (MWP), experiencing the warmest weather in the last 700 years (Figure 10.1). Of course, the weather in the Alps during the winter was not anything approaching warm, but it did mean that winter travel over the Alps was at least possible. The party consisted of several bishops, a strong contingent of soldiers for protection, and probably a dozen or more ladies in waiting. Their progress through France, therefore, was predictably slow. They managed to reach the village of Briançon on the French side of the Alps in December, spending Christmas a few miles from the Col de Montgenèvre pass that would take them over the Alps.

They hired local guides called *marons* whose business was helping travelers safely traverse the Montgenèvre pass. Although much of the journey could be made on horseback, when the snow grew too deep or the path too steep, the party had to walk their horses. The trip up the pass was hard enough, but the trip down into Italy was even harder. In places, the road became so steep that walking was impossible. In that case, their guides strapped the travelers onto sleds and used ropes to ease them down the slope. The horses had to be lowered in the same way. During their descent, the relatively warm weather worked against them. The snow melted at midday, making the track dangerously slippery. Nevertheless, the party managed the crossing, arriving at a hostelry in the foothills of the Italian Alps in January.

After resting, the party continued south to Rome and then to Naples where they had expected to go by ship to Sicily. However, a diplomatic crisis caused by the death of the Holy Roman Emperor Frederick Barbarosa forestalled that plan, and they continued south by land, arriving in Sicily after the start of Lent. Berengaria and Richard couldn't be married until they arrived in Cyprus after Lent was over. After the wedding, Berengaria was crowned, the only Queen of England to have been crowned in Cyprus, and the only English Queen who never set foot in England.

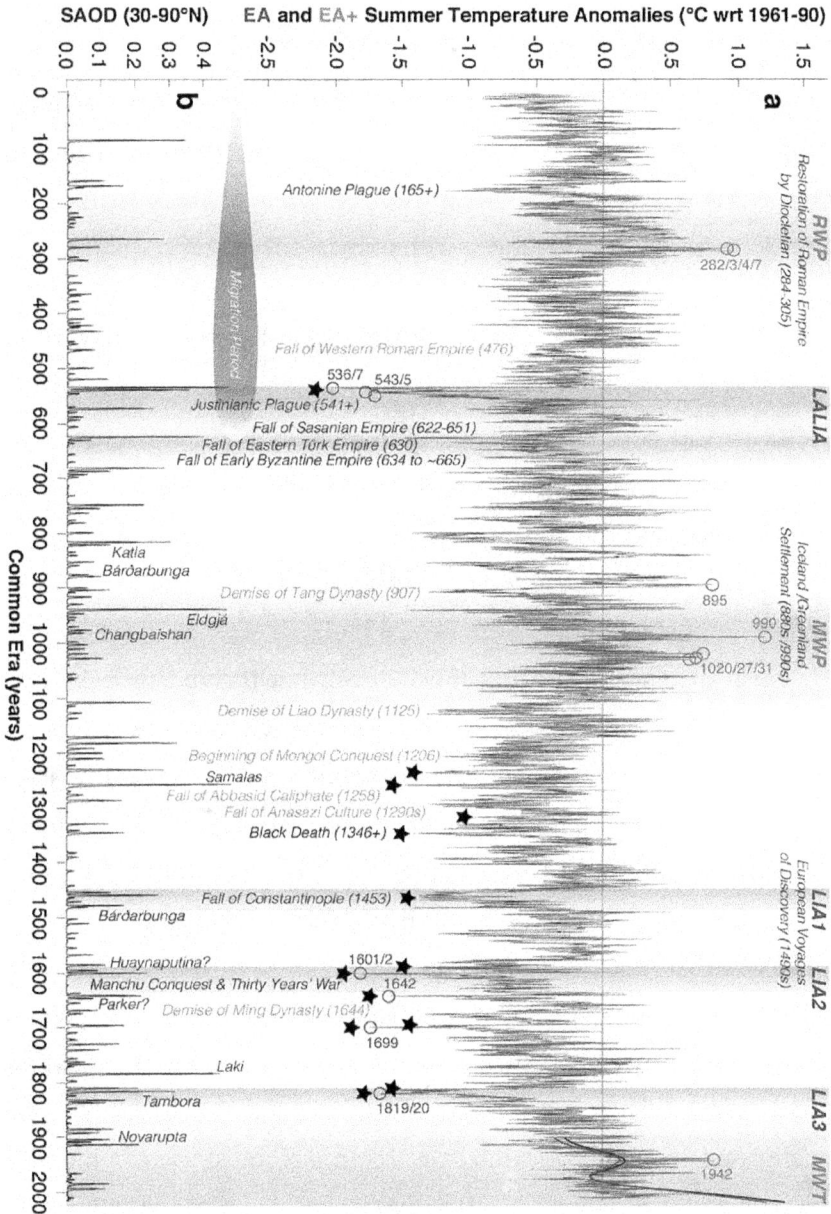

Figure 10.1 Temperature extremes and major volcanic events between 1 and 2000 CE. (a) The three warmest intervals, the Roman Warm Period (RWP), Medieval Warm Period (MWP), and the Modern Warm Time (MWT), also the four coldest intervals, the Late Antique Little Ice Age (LALIA) and three periods of the Little Ice Age (LIA1, LIA2, LIA3), and (b) major volcanic events. Reprinted from Büntgen et al., 2020[1], an open-access journal.

⇔

The Medieval Warm Period was a relatively prosperous time for most of Europe. By 1250 CE it had warmed up to the point that wine grapes were being grown in northern England. The warm weather certainly helped agricultural production, but several technological advances also improved agricultural production. These included the use of the horse collar, the invention of waterwheel and windmill technology, and the institution of a three-field rotation system for crops. For the 90% of the population engaged mainly in agriculture, life wasn't exactly easy, but it was much better than it had been during the colder Migration Age and the subsequent Dark Ages. Famines still happened periodically when adverse weather lowered crop yields, but compared to earlier centuries, things were not so bad.

It wasn't only agricultural production that thrived in Europe. For the top-ten percent of the population (church clerics, knights, and the nobility) the Medieval Warm Period was a time of cultural renaissance as well. Prior to the eleventh century, Latin was the principal language of the written word in Europe. But by the thirteenth century, a vernacular literature predominantly written in French, had become popular. Geoffrey of Monmouth's *History of the Kings of Britain*, completed in 1138 CE, introduced King Arthur to the reading public. Since many of the nobility were still illiterate, the stories were mostly read aloud to them. The twelfth-century French writer Chrétien de Troyes added Lancelot and the Holy Grail to the King Arthur stories, which made them even more popular. Courtly love—the idea that men and women could actually fall in love with each other instead of just having procreative sex—was invented. Troubadours wrote songs extolling the virtues of knights who loved highborn women chastely (or not so chastely) from afar. At the Cathedral of Notre Dame in Paris, composers were experimenting with music consisting of many different independent melodies (polyphony), not the single melody (monophony) that had dominated western music for eight hundred years. More ominously, the population of Europe had literally exploded in the Medieval Warm Period. England's population had increased from about 1.4 million in 1066 CE to more than five million by 1300 CE. All in all, life was pretty good.

But things were about to change. Another climate reversal, known as the Little Ice Age (LIA) was on its way.

$$\Longleftrightarrow$$

The beginning of the LIA around the year 1300 CE was characterized by a noticeable cooling of summer temperatures (Fig. 10.1). However, during the cooler spring of 1315 CE, it rained in much of Europe, and it was a lot of rain indeed. One chronicler named Bernardo Guidonis wrote, *Exceedingly great rains descended from the heavens, and they made huge and deep mud-pools on the land.*[1] The rain began seven weeks after Easter and continued without letup for the most critical part of the growing season between May and July. The rains abated somewhat in August and September, but the weather remained unseasonably cool. The cool weather prevented the surviving crops from ripening, and much of the harvest in the year 1315 CE was lost. The spring of 1316 CE was almost as wet as the previous year, and again there was widespread crop failure. The resulting "Great Famine" saw tens of thousands of people dying of starvation or disease.[1] It was truly one of the most wretched times in human history, and it was a direct result of the climate reversal from a warming period to a cooling period. The LIA lingered on for more than five hundred years until the Modern Warm Time commenced about the year 1860 CE (Fig. 10.1).

What initiated the LIA in the first place, what caused it to linger for so long, and what caused the Modern Warm Time that ended it? While climatologists have many ideas about answers to those questions, there is still no firm scholarly consensus as to the ultimate cause(s). There is, however, a broad consensus that the LIA most likely reflected a complex interaction between multiple tectonic, atmospheric, and oceanic processes, different kinds of "forcing" events that resulted in rapid but transient cooling, and positive feedback loops that served to prolong the duration of the cooling.[2]

For many years it was thought that the LIA was caused primarily by a decrease in solar radiation reaching the earth. Modern insolation records based on isotopic measurements (Figure 10.2) do show a rapid dip around the year 1300 CE, which certainly suggests it as causative factor in beginning the LIA.[3] That same record, however, indicates a number of dips that occurred during the LIA time frame (1300-1860 CE), suggesting that decreasing solar radiation was also a factor in prolonging the LIA.

But as accurately dated information from ice cores, sediment cores, and tree rings became available, several researchers pointed toward volcanic activity as a triggering factor for the LIA as well.[1,4,5,6,7] Beginning with the massive Samalas volcanic eruption of 1257 CE, there were a series of smaller but still significant volcanic eruptions between the late thirteenth and the nineteenth centuries. It's interesting to contrast the numbers and intensities of the recorded volcanic eruptions between 100 and 400 CE when it was predominantly warm (Roman Warm Period), and those recorded from 1257 CE and 1900 CE when it became cooler. Visually, it certainly looks like there was more volcanic activity during the LALIA and LIA periods than during the Roman Warm Period (Fig. 10.1), and that difference is statistically significant.[1,4]

It wasn't only the sulfur aerosols in the atmosphere that seem to have sustained the LIA over such a long time. In 1993, a team led by

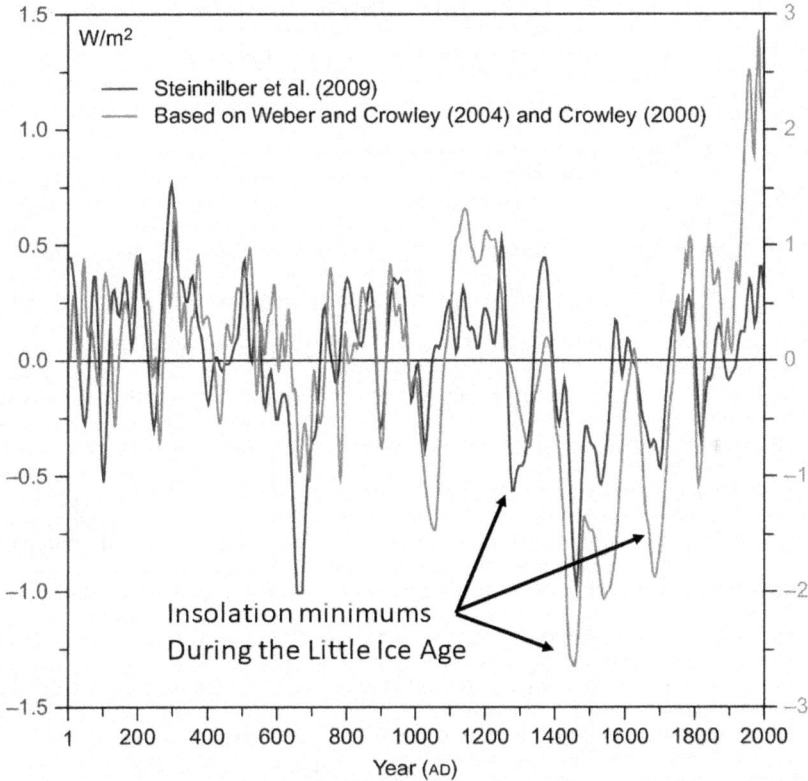

Figure 10.2. Reconstructions of total solar irradiance reaching the earth in the last 2,000 years. The record by Steinhilber et al. (2009) is based on the ¹⁰Be record. The red line is based on the ¹⁴C record in tree rings in 0-1000 and on ¹⁰Be thereafter. Note the different scaling for both curves. Modified from Luterbacher et al., 2012[3].

Gerard Bond of the Lamont-Doherty Earth Observatory used a correlation between air temperatures over the Greenland ice cap over the last 90,000 years with seafloor sediment cores collected in the North Atlantic Ocean to demonstrate that a series of rapid warm-cold oscillations had occurred over the last 90,000 years.[8] Each cooling cycle was punctuated by an enormous discharge of icebergs into the ocean, an event followed by an abrupt shift to a warmer climate. One indicator of the sea-surface temperature was the abundance of a planktonic foraminifera that lives in seawaters cooler than 10°C. This abundance is a good indicator because when summer temperatures are less than 5°C that species of foraminifera comprises about 95% of all the organisms present in the sediments. Furthermore, these cold-warm cycles were observed to occur every 1,500 years or so.

If these warm-cold cycles occur with such regularity, it seemed unlikely that volcanic activity was the only factor triggering the cycles. The discharge of icebergs at the end of each cooling cycle indicated that something else might be going on. Evidence of what that might be was provided by the fact that the Modern Warm Time led to the lateral recession of ice-cap margins in the Arctic of Canada.[4] The recession of the ice exposed plant remains that had been killed by the ice accumulation at the beginning of the LIA (~1300 CE). The ^{14}C composition of the plant material, collected between 2005 and 2010, accurately dates the time when the snowline dropped below the collection site. Interestingly, there was no record of ice accumulating between 950 and 1250 CE, which correlates nicely with the Medieval Warm Period.

Many of the kill-dates cluster between 1275 and 1300 CE, suggesting an abrupt summer temperature decrease in the late thirteenth century.[4] Those dates coincide with an interval of four large volcanic events (Fig. 10.1). Given the fact that temperature decreases associated with volcanic events are typically transient (one-three years), what could explain the colder temperatures that preserved the ice into the twenty-first century? One explanation is that the cold snaps following the volcanic eruptions would have increased export of ice from the Arctic glaciers. That ice export could have led to a freshening and vertical stratification of the North Atlantic, which in turn could weaken ocean currents that transport heat from lower to higher latitudes.[4] A more recent paper even suggests, based on sediment-core data, that a "Great Sea-Ice Anomaly" occurred at approximately 1300 CE, which may have initiated the LIA without the involvement of "volcanic forcing."[9]

Thus far, possible causes of the LIA include a lowering of solar irradiation, volcanic episodes which produced a temporary further lowering of solar irradiation, and ice export from the Arctic to the North Atlantic. The last one we'll consider (although there are more) is the export of cold seawater from the North Atlantic to the Southern Ocean via deep ocean currents. Because cold seawater is denser than warm seawater, cold seawater in the North Atlantic sinks to the ocean bottom and moves southward. This North Atlantic Deep Water (NADW) is an important driver of worldwide ocean currents, including the Gulf Stream, which then carries warm seawater from the Southern Ocean northward.

But temperature is not the only factor that affects the density of seawater. It turns out that the Pacific Ocean is less salty than the Atlantic Ocean. This lower salinity reflects evaporation in the Atlantic Ocean, the westward transport of this moisture to the Pacific Ocean, and its deposition via rainfall.[10] The salinity of North Atlantic water therefore increases over time, gradually becoming denser. When the density reaches a tipping point, it triggers an episode of higher NADW export to the south.[11] That export could cause surface currents like the Gulf Stream to transport more warm seawater north, leading to a moderating northern climate (Medieval Warm Period). However, when the salinity of North Atlantic water has been sufficiently lowered, export of NADW southward decreases, thereby decreasing the northward transport of warm water. These occurrences could lead to a cooling trend in the Northern Hemisphere like during the LIA.

Geochemical evidence from a variety of sources suggests that the average periodicity of this mechanism would be between 1,000 and 2000 years. One of these lines of evidence was reported by geologist Gerald Bond in 1999.[12] When examining sediments cored from the floor of the North Atlantic, he noticed that the sand and gravel grains were much coarser than sediments that could have been transported by ocean currents. That indicated the sediments had been rafted out to sea by icebergs from Arctic glaciers. Secondly, the proportion of iron-stained sand grains varied over time. He knew that some of the Arctic glaciers advanced over red-stained sandstones where the ice would have picked up iron-stained sand grains. The varied proportion pointed to a periodicity in the delivery of ice-rafted sediments (Figure 10.3). That periodicity, in turn, may reflect less ice-rafting during warmer periods (fewer icebergs) and more during cold periods (more icebergs). Note the elevated concentrations of iron-stained grains that occurred about 1500 years ago (roughly the beginning of the Late Antique Little Ice Age) and about 1000 years ago (roughly the beginning of the Little Ice Age). While these findings are certainly not definitive proof, they are nonetheless interesting.

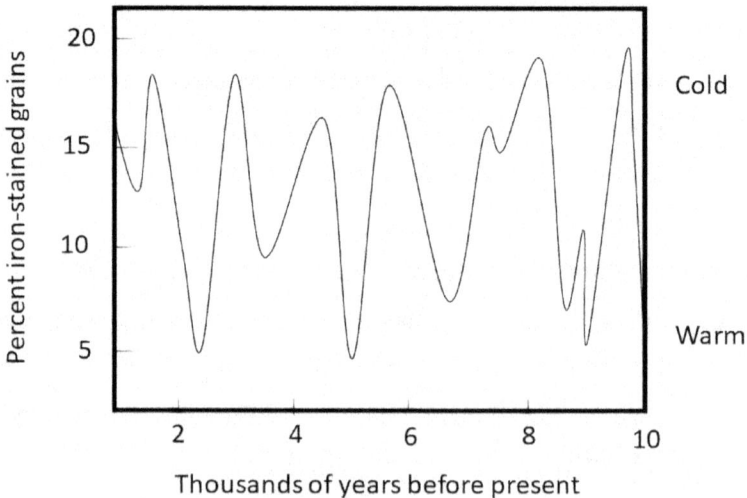

Figure 10.3. Climatic oscillations over the last 10,000 years with iron-stained sand grains as a proxy for water temperature. Data is from Bond et al., 1999.[12]

The beginning of the LIA around 1300 CE was a disaster for Europe. The greatly expanded population generated by the Medieval Warm Period, combined with cooler temperatures that inevitably lowered agricultural production, led to food shortages. Conditions worsened in 1315 CE when a wave of cold rain swept down on Europe and continued for two years. Between the cold and the rain, agriculture virtually ceased and precipitated what historians now call The Great Famine. Gruesome stories about parents abandoning their children, older people deliberately starved, and human cannibalism are told but difficult to document. What can be documented, however, is that 15%-20% of the European population died during the Great Famine.

Although weather abated somewhat in 1317 CE, because most of the cattle and draft animals (as well as seed corn) had been consumed, the famine persisted for years after that. It's possible that the period of cold, wet weather was caused at least in part by the eruption of the Tarawera volcano in New Zealand that began erupting about the year 1315 CE.[13] More likely, it was some unlucky combination of volcanic activity, periodic changes in sea-ice in the Northern Atlantic Ocean, and decreased solar radiation that led to the disaster.

Once again the clear historical lesson is that a sustained warm period causing population growth, followed by a climate reversal that decreases agricultural production, is a recipe for disaster to human societies.

REFERENCES

1. Büntgen, U., Arseneault, D., Boucher, É., Churakova, O.V., Gennaretti, F., Crivellaro, A., Hughes, M.K., Kirdyanov, A.V., Klippel, L., Krusic, P.J. and Linderholm, H.W., 2020. Prominent role of volcanism in Common Era climate variability and human history. Dendrochronologia, 64, p.125757.

2. Fagan, Brian. 2000. The Little Ice Age. Basic Books, New York, New York. 246 pp.

3. Luterbacher, J., García-Herrera, R., Acker-On, S., Allen, R., Alvarez-Castro, M.C., Benito, G., Booth, J., Buntgen, U., Cagatay, N., Colombaroli, D. and Davis, B., 2012. A review of 2000 years of paleoclimatic evidence in the Mediterranean.

4. Hegerl, G.C., Crowley, T.J., Baum, S.K., Kim, K.Y. and Hyde, W.T., 2003. Detection of volcanic, solar and greenhouse gas signals in paleo-reconstructions of Northern Hemispheric temperature. Geophysical Research Letters, 30(5).

5. Crowley, T.J., Zielinski, G., Vinther, B., Udisti, R., Kreutz, K., Cole-Dai, J. and Castellano, E., 2008. Volcanism and the little ice age. PAGES news, 16(2), pp.22-23.

6. Miller, G.H., Geirsdóttir, Á., Zhong, Y., Larsen, D.J., Otto-Bliesner, B.L., Holland, M.M., Bailey, D.A., Refsnider, K.A., Lehman, S.J., Southon, J.R. and Anderson, C., 2012. Abrupt onset of the Little Ice Age triggered by volcanism and sustained by sea-ice/ocean feedbacks. Geophysical Research Letters, 39(2).

7. Schleussner, C.F. and Feulner, G., 2013. A volcanically triggered regime shift in the subpolar North Atlantic Ocean as a possible origin of the Little Ice Age. Climate of the Past, 9(3), pp.1321-1330.

8. Bond, G., Broecker, W., Johnsen, S., McManus, J., Labeyrie, L., Jouzel, J. and Bonani, G., 1993. Correlations between climate records from North Atlantic sediments and Greenland ice. Nature, 365(6442), pp.143-147.

9. Miles, M.W., Andresen, C.S. and Dylmer, C.V., 2020. Evidence for extreme export of Arctic sea ice leading the abrupt onset of the Little Ice Age. Science advances, 6(38), p.eaba4320.

10. Dey, D. and Döös, K., 2020. Atmospheric freshwater transport from the Atlantic to the Pacific Ocean: A Lagrangian analysis. Geophysical Research Letters, 47(6), p.e2019GL086176.

11. Broecker, W.S., 2001. Was the medieval warm period global? Science, 291(5508), pp.1497-1499.

12. G. C. Bond et al., 1999. The North Atlantic's 1-2 kyr climate rhythm: Relation to Heinrich events, Dansgaard/Oeschger cycles and the Little Ice Age. Mechanisms of Global Climate Change at Millennial Time Scales, Geophysical Monograph Series, vol. 112 American Geophysical Union, Washington D.C. pp. 35-58.

13. Nairn, I.A., Shane, P.R., Cole, J.W., Leonard, G.J., Self, S. and Pearson, N., 2004. Rhyolite magma processes of the ~AD 1315 Kaharoa eruption episode, Tarawera volcano, New Zealand. Journal of Volcanology and Geothermal Research, 131(3-4), pp.265-294.

CHAPTER 11
Global cooling and the Russian Time of Troubles

THE COOLING TRENDS THAT ENDED the Late Bronze Age, the Roman Warm Period, and the Medieval Warm Period certainly contributed to the famines, epidemics, and the political instability that followed. The written record, however, is sparse enough that historians still debate the contribution of cooling climate to that political instability. By 1600 CE, well into the Renaissance, the connection between political instability in Russia following a sudden cooling event is more compelling.

The people who called themselves the Rus', predecessors of modern Russians, seem to have originated in what is now eastern Sweden in the eighth century CE. The name Rus' probably derived from the Finnic name for Sweden (Ruotsi), which in turn comes from an Old Norse term that means "the men who row." Traveling by boat was the easiest means of transportation in the heavily forested land of Northern Europe in the eighth century. According to the twelfth-century Primary Chronicle written by Saint Nestor in 862 CE, a chieftain named Rurik was invited to rule the Rus' from a stronghold named Novgorod (new fort). This was the founding of the Rurik Dynasty that ruled over a loose confederation of Slavic, Baltic, and Finnic peoples in northeastern Europe now called Kievan Rus' by scholars.

The Rurik Dynasty lasted for more than 700 years. Its demise was largely the work of Ivan IV (The Terrible), the first Muscovite to bear the title Tsar. The word "tsar" is derived from the Latin "Caesar" because Ivan claimed decent from the Roman emperor Augustus. Ivan the Terrible, however, had serious anger-management issues that included killing his twenty-six-year-old son and heir during an argument in 1581 CE. That death led to the crowning of another son named Fyodor Tsar when Ivan died in 1584 CE. Fyodor, unfortunately, was mentally impaired and incapable of ruling. The ruling of Russia fell to Fyodor's brother-in-law Boris Godunov, who promptly claimed the throne when Fyodor died in 1598 CE, ending the Rurik dynasty. This event was sure to cause political trouble.

It turned out to be very bad timing for Boris Godunov. Two years into Godunov's reign in February 1600 CE, the Huaynaputina Volcano located in southern Peru erupted explosively.[1] It was the largest volcanic eruption in South America in the last 2,000 years, the volume of ash ejected was about 30 km^3, and it registered a Volcanic Explosivity Index (VEI) of 6. VEI is a measure of a volcano's destructiveness, ranging from 1 to 8, based on the volume, duration, and height of material expulsed during an eruptive phase, with higher numbers indicating more destructive eruptions. By way of comparison, the Mount St. Helens eruption in 1980 ejected just 4.2 km^3 of ash with a VEI of 5. More importantly for the world's climate, the Huaynaputina eruption released between twenty-six and fifty-five million tons of sulfur and sulfur aerosols into the atmosphere.[2] Those aerosols immediately began reducing solar radiation reaching the earth, and the winter of 1601 CE was the coldest in Europe in the last 600 years. This record-cold was a disaster for Russia. Widespread crop failures and the resulting famine killed more than 500,000 people, fully one third of Russia's population between 1601 and 1603 CE. This was the beginning of the Time of Troubles, which lasted until 1613 CE.

Politically, this time was also a disaster for Boris Godunov. He had come to the throne as the first non-Rurik Tsar in more than 700 years.

Since he claimed the throne by way of marriage instead of descent, and because he almost certainly had Tsar Fyodor's younger brother Dmitry murdered, he was widely seen as a usurper. Many Russians blamed the terrible famine, the worst in Russian history, as being divine retribution for Godunov's murderous usurpation. When a man came forward claiming to be Dmitry, and thus the rightful Tsar, the Russians were more than willing to suspend credulity and believe this first "false Dmitry." Two more false Dmitrys followed.

The uncertainty in Russia following the famine was viewed as a political opportunity by Russia's neighbor to the west, the Polish-Lithuanian Commonwealth, who promptly invaded Russia to place the first false Dmitry on the throne. During the war that followed the invasion, Godunov died unexpectedly in 1605 CE. With the support of the Polish and Lithuanians, the first false Dmitry was placed on the throne, and Moscow was occupied by Polish troops. That false Dmitry was murdered in 1606 CE by a Russian named Vasili IV Shuysky who then claimed the Tsardom. He was unable to stem the chaos. The Tatars invaded from the south and the Swedes invaded from the north. Gangs of Polish soldiers roamed the countryside robbing, raping, and killing peasants. Two more false Dmitrys turned up when Shuysky was driven from power, and in all there were six claimants to the Tsardom between 1598 and 1613 CE. Finally, the Russian Zemsky Sobor (Assembly of the Land) elected Mikhail Romanov Tsar in 1613 CE, and the Time of Troubles began to fade.

Was the political instability of the Time of Troubles caused by the Huaynaputina Volcano and the climate reversal that followed? Let's imagine what might have happened if Huaynaputina had *not* exploded in February 1600 CE. Ivan the Terrible would still have murdered his son and heir in 1581 CE, which doomed the simpleminded son Fyodor to become Tsar in 1584 CE. Fyodor's sister would still have married Boris Godunov, and Godunov would still have become regent for Fyodor. When Fyodor died in 1598 CE, Godunov, by virtue of his marriage would have still become Tsar, and he would have likely still murdered Dmitry. Without Huaynaputina, there wouldn't have been a famine that could be blamed on Godunov. But when Godunov died in 1605 CE, there still would have been a succession struggle because of the Rurik Dynasty's demise. The succession struggle still could have motivated the Polish-Lithuanian Commonwealth, the Swedes, and the Golden Horde Tatars to invade Russia, more than enough to cause a "time of troubles." So no, it's probably not correct to say the Huayna-putina explosion "caused" the Time of Troubles. There were plenty of troubles around already, but Huaynaputina certainly worsened things. When a country loses one third of its population to famine, a famine that would have been much milder without Huaynaputina, it certainly magnifies the other troubles. As we've seen before, it was an unlucky combination of factors that "caused" the Time of Troubles.

Nonetheless, Huaynaputina did happen, and it didn't just affect Russia.[3] In France, the date of the beginning of the wine harvest for 1601 CE is among the seven latest from 1500 to 1700 CE.[4] In Germany, wine production for the year 1602 CE was less than 5% of the average value of the previous and following seventy-five years.[5] In Sweden, record amounts of snow in the winter of 1601 CE were followed in the spring by the worst floods in memory. The resulting harvest was very poor, which led to hunger and disease.[6] In China, there was a seventeen-day difference in the blossoming dates of peach trees in Hangzhou between 1601 and 1602 CE.[7] In Japan, the official date of the freezing of Lake Suwa in central Japan, known as Omiwatari, has been recorded for more than 500 years[8], and 1601 CE represents one of the four earliest dates for this phenomenon between 1520 and 1680 CE. In the United States, there is an unusual sedimentary layer in the Santa Barbara

Basin in California, dated at 1605 CE ± 5 years. This layer has been interpreted as evidence for intense precipitation and regional flooding associated with an interval of rapid, pronounced cooling.[9]

By virtue of its extraordinary power, the volume of sulfur injected into the atmosphere, and the demonstrated effects of the earth's climate for at least three years after the explosion, Huaynaputina is one of the best-documented climate reversals in historic times. Although Huayna-putina exploded during the Little Ice Age, the fifty years leading up to 1600 CE were a time of gradual warming (Fig. 10.1). Once again, the historical pattern is one of gradual warming, increased agricultural production, and population growth punctuated almost instantly by an abrupt cooling trend. That cooling trend, as usual, produced extreme hardships for earth's human populations, with political instability cer-tainly one of those hardships.

The obvious question is how likely is it that, with the earth now in a conspicuous period of global warming, with a population nearing eight billion people, that another Huaynaputina-like event will cause an abrupt climate reversal? Unfortunately, the answer is that it is not only likely but also inevitable. The reason for that assessment stems from the present state of Earth's plate tectonics. The Pacific Ocean is presently surrounded by advancing continent-bearing plates whose movements are shrinking the Pacific basin. Because continental crust is lighter than oceanic crust, the oceanic crust is subducted beneath the continents where it partially melts (Figure 11.1). The magma pro-duced by this partial melting then ascends upwards, causing volcanos to erupt. Moreover, because partial melting produces magma that is rather viscous, a great deal of pressure can build up within the magma chamber. When the top of the chamber finally fails, it causes an explo-sion of ash and gas that, like Huaynaputina, can be hugely destructive.

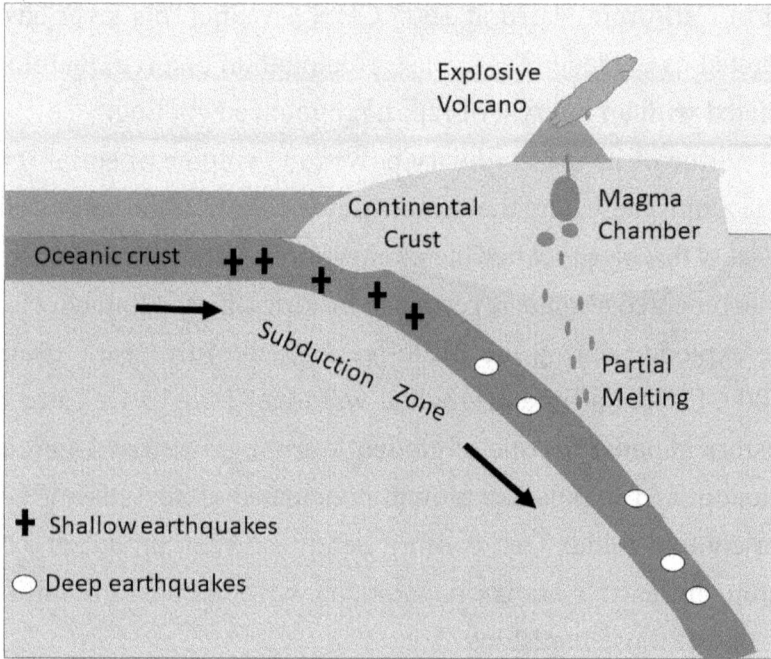

Figure 11.1. Oceanic crust being subducted beneath continental crust producing both shallow and deep earthquakes with the production of viscous magma that rises to the surface to form explosive volcanos.

The Pacific basin is encircled by subduction zones, all of which are producing potentially explosive volcanos. More than 900 volcanos in this so-called Ring of Fire (Figure 11.2) have erupted in the last 10,000 years. That is the principal reason why, despite the present period of global warming, there are bound to be future climate reversals "triggered" by explosive Ring of Fire volcanos. Just how badly those climate reversals will affect human society depends in part on how they interact with the other solar, orbital, tectonic, atmospheric, and oceanic processes that affect climate change.

It also depends on how prepared human societies will be to withstand the effects of those climate reversals.

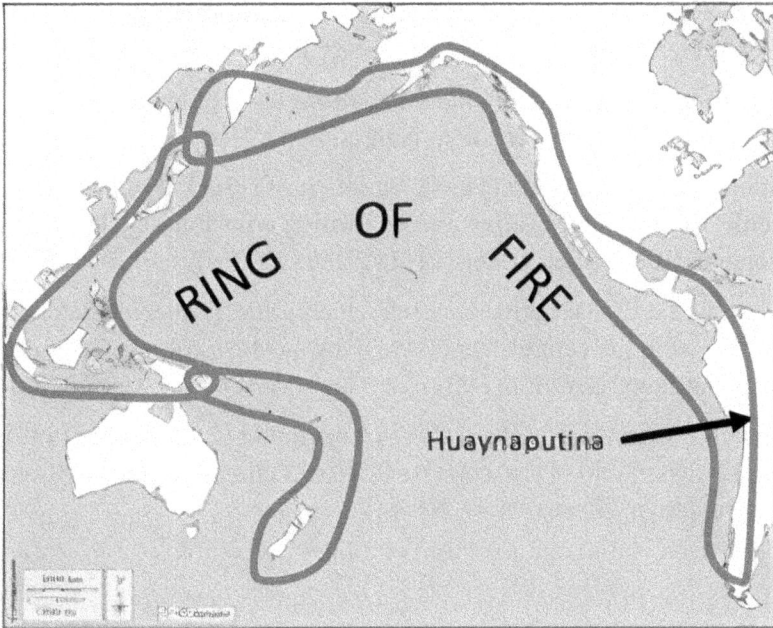

Figure 11.2. Map showing the present-day Ring of Fire and the location of Huaynaputina.

REFERENCES

1. Fei, J., Zhang, D.D. and Lee, H.F., 2016. 1600 AD Huaynaputina eruption (Peru), abrupt cooling, and epidemics in China and Korea. Advances in Meteorology, 2016.

2. Costa, F., Scaillet, B. and Gourgaud, A., 2003. Massive atmospheric sulfur loading of the AD 1600 Huaynaputina eruption and implications for petrologic sulfur estimates. Geophysical Research Letters, 30(2).

3. Verosub, K.L. and Lippman, J., 2008. Global impacts of the 1600 eruption of Peru's Huaynaputina volcano. Eos, Transactions American Geophysical Union, 89(15), pp.141-142.

4. Chuine, I., P. Yiou, N. Viovy, B. Seguin, V. Daux, and E. Le Roy Ladurie (2004), Grape ripening as an indicator of past climate, Nature, 432, 289–290.

5. Warde, P. (2006), Ecology, Economy and State Formation in Early Modern Germany, Cambridge University Press, New York.

6. Utterström, G. (1955), Climatic fluctuations and population problems in early modern history, Scandinavian Economic History Revue 3, 26–41.

7. Hameed, S., and G. Gong (1994), Variation of spring climate in lower-middle Yangtse River Valley and its relation with solar-cycle length, Geophysical Research Letters 21(24), 2693–2996.

8. Arakawa, H. (1954), Fujiwhara on five centuries of freezing dates of Lake Suwa in the central Japan, Archives of Meteorology, Geophysics, Bioklimatology, Ser. B, 6(1-2), 152–166.

9. Schimmelmann, A., M. Zhao, C. C. Harvey, and C. B. Lange (1998), A large California flood and correlative global climatic events 400 years ago, Quaternary Research 49, 51–61.

CHAPTER 12

The Battle of Waterloo, and the Near Extinction of Humanity

THE NIGHT PRECEDING THE CLIMACTIC Battle of Waterloo on June 18, 1815, was equally unpleasant for the British, their Dutch and Prussian allies, and the opposing French troops. For one thing, it rained most of the night, and none of the soldiers, and few of the officers, had any shelter. By morning, all 185,000 combatants were soaked and thoroughly miserable. That wasn't the worst of it. Being late June, the weather had been uncomfortably warm the day before, but when the rain swept in, the temperature cooled abruptly, probably dropping below 60°F. In addition to being soaked, the soldiers were cold. All of this was to have a profound effect on the outcome of the coming battle.

These abnormally cool temperatures, however, may have been the natural result of a global cooling event triggered by the violent eruption of a volcano, known as Mount Tambora, on the island of Sumbawa in Indonesia. The eruption had a Volcanic Explosive Index (VEI) of 7, just below the highest recorded value of VEI-8, and it is the second-largest volcanic event to have occurred in written human history. It released approximately 44 cubic kilometers of ejected material, creating an atmospheric plume of ash and sulfur aerosols that reached an altitude of 148,000 feet. The eruptions began on April 5, 1815, and culminated in massive explosions on April 10 that were heard on the island of Ternate 870 miles away.

There's no question that the inclement weather the night before

Waterloo greatly affected its outcome. A more intriguing question is could the explosion of Mount Tambora have contributed to the rainfall and cool temperatures at Waterloo, half a world away? The last day of the battle, after all, was only two months after the April 10 explosions. Nevertheless, it probably would have been enough time for the ash and sulfur aerosol plume in the stratosphere to reach Belgium from Indonesia. When Mount Pinatubo erupted in the Philippines in 1991, the ash plume circumnavigated the globe in less than a month[1]. It's not impossible that the plume contributed to the unusually cool and wet weather experienced in Europe in the spring of 1815.

The chemical effects of ash and sulfur plumes are not the only ways that volcanic eruptions can affect the atmosphere. Specifically, some of the energy released by volcanic eruptions is converted into electrical charges that give individual ash particles a net negative charge, giving the ash plume itself a net negative charge. While those charges decay fairly rapidly (between two and twenty minutes), for a time negatively charged ash particles exist in a negatively charged electrical field (the ash plume). That serves to "levitate" ash particles much higher into the ionosphere than would be possible simply by thermal transport.[2]

In addition, the electrical field of the atmosphere is involved with cloud formation. That being the case, significant disruption of the atmospheric electrical field would likely disturb cloud formation, resulting initially in lower cloud cover and precipitation. These effects contrast with *increased* precipitation in the vicinity of erupting volcanos due to the plume's high sulfur aerosol load. However, as the ionosphere recovers its electrical balance in the weeks following an eruption, cloud formation would resume in a now-moister atmosphere, possibly causing unusually intense rainfall. May and June 1815 were unusually wet in Europe following Tambora's eruption in April. That unseasonable weather might reflect the initial suppression and subsequent recovery of cloud formation owing to the electrostatic levitation of volcanic ash.[2]

None of this prove that the clouds and rainfall on the eve of the final Battle of the Waterloo campaign were caused by Tambora's eruption. But it is interesting that the weather was unusual enough that some of the battle's participants were motivated to record what they saw. One of these was a Private William Wheeler (51st Kings Yorkshire Infantry) who recorded what he saw and heard in the afternoon of June 17[3].

> ....and as it began to rain the road soon became very
> heavy...the rain increased, the thunder and lightning
> approached nearer...with...repeated bright flashes of
> lightning attended with tremendous volleys of thunder that
> shook the very earth....

Even more illuminating was a description of the unusual cloud formations seen prior to the arrival of the rain given by a British Captain of Artillery named Alexander Mercer:

> The sky had become overcast since the morning, and at this
> moment presented a most extraordinary appearance. Large
> isolated masses of a thunder cloud, of the deepest most inky
> black, their lower edges hard and strongly defined, lagging
> down, as if momentarily about to burst, involving our
> position and everything on it in deep and gloomy obscurity.

⇔

Speculating how a volcanic eruption may have affected the Battle of Waterloo, and thus the future of all of Europe, is interesting and entertaining. What is not speculation, however, is the profound effects that Tambora's eruption had on the weather in Europe[1], the United States[3], and Asia[4] for at least the next ten years. In actuality, it wasn't solely the Tambora eruption. Several other volcanic eruptions were also involved. In December 1808, meteorological observations by two South Americans describe a stratospheric aerosol haze, a "transparent cloud that obstructs the sun's brilliance," that was visible over the city of Bogotá, Colombia, from December 11, 1808, to at least mid-February 1809. A physician in Lima, Peru, describes sunset after-glows (akin to well-documented examples known to be caused by stratospheric volcanic sulfur aerosols) from mid-December 1808 to February 1809. This event, known as the *Unknown Eruption* because its location has not yet been identified, is the second-most-explosive sulfur-rich volcanic eruption (next to Tambora) in the last two centuries.[5] In 1812, there were eruptions of the La Soufrière (which means "the sulfur mine") volcano on the Island of Saint Vincent in the Caribbean[6], and the Mount Awu volcano, which is near Tambora in Indonesia. When Tambora exploded in 1815, significant amounts of sulfur aerosols were already present in the upper atmosphere.

Other things going on during that time were affecting the global climate as well. Between about 1790 and 1830 was a period of unusually low solar sunspot activity known as the Dalton Minimum. Low sunspot activity reduces the amount of solar radiation reaching the earth, and that reduction alone could have cooled global temperatures. Put together with the period of unusually vigorous volcanic activity between 1808 and 1815, the results were predictable. The decade following 1810 was the coldest and longest-sustained period of below-average hemispheric and tropical temperatures in the last 500 years.[3]

Also predictable was the effect of those colder temperatures on agricultural production in the United States, Europe, and Asia. A historian from Massachusetts named William Atkins later (1887) wrote:[7]

> *Severe frosts occurred every month; June 7th and 8th snow*
> *fell, and it was so cold that crops were cut down, even*
> *freezing the roots ... In the early Autumn when corn was in*

*the milk it was so thoroughly frozen that it never ripened
and was scarcely worth harvesting. Breadstuffs were scarce
and prices high and the poorer class of people were often
in straits for want of food. It must be remembered that the
granaries of the great west had not then been opened to us
by railroad communication, and people were obliged to rely
upon their own resources or upon others in their immediate
locality.*

Things were just as bad in western and central Europe. A gentleman named Carl von Clausewitz happened to be touring the Prussian Rhineland in the spring of 1817, and he reported a really horrifying scene:[8]

*The author, who traveled on horseback through the Eifel
region in spring 1817, where he passed the night in villages
and little towns, often had a heartrending view of this
misery, because these areas belong to the poorest classes in
the land. He saw ruined figures, scarcely resembling men,
prowling around the fields searching for food among the
unharvested and already half rotten potatoes that never
grew to maturity.*

In addition to starvation was the rapid spread of disease. An epidemic of typhus broke out in Europe in 1816 to be followed by an epidemic of cholera in 1817. The cholera pandemic of 1817-1824 began in Calcutta, India, and quickly spread throughout Asia, eventually reaching Europe. These epidemics were worsened by the weakened state of undernourished people as well as the unsanitary conditions brought on by poverty.

The larger point is how much of this suffering was directly related to the climate reversal brought on by the combination of explosive volcanic eruptions between 1808 and 1815 and the Dalton Minimum of 1790 to 1830. It's also worth noting that, while the weather was clearly cooler during the period 1810 to 1819, average summer temperatures in western and central Europe were only 1° C - 3° C cooler than mean temperatures between 1951 and 1970.[8] The obvious conclusion is that a short-term climate reversal of just one or two degrees can have devastating effects on human populations. That might have happened 73,500 years ago.[9]

The first inkling that the human population might have suffered a precipitous decline, commonly referred to as a "bottleneck," that occurred prior to 60,000 years ago comes from a study of human mitochondrial DNA, or mtDNA.[10] MtDNA is present only in mitochondria, the energy-producing organelles in human cells. MtDNA is particularly well-suited for studying genetic changes over time because it is inherited only through the female line. Nuclear DNA, on the other hand, is inherited 50-50 from each male-female pair, and is thus recombined in each successive generation. That recombination makes it difficult to trace individual mutations that accumulate in DNA over time. Also, mtDNA accumulates mutations faster than nuclear DNA. The lack of recombination and the faster mutation rate of mtDNA makes it a useful "clock" for tracing genetic changes over time.

When mutations of mtDNA in different modern human populations (Australian, African, Asian, European, and Papua New Guinean) were examined closely[11], they indicated that the human line originated in Africa around 200,000 years ago. Beginning about 100,000 years ago, humans spread out of Africa into separate regions, but there doesn't seem to have been a dramatic increase in overall populations. Sometime before 60,000 years ago, human populations around the world experienced a sudden "bottleneck," with overall numbers of humans worldwide decreasing to between 3,000 and 10,000 individuals.[8] What could possibly have caused such a disastrous conflagration?

We've already seen from the 1815 eruption of Tambora what a VEI of 7 can do, sparking a wave of famines and epidemics that affected people all over the world[8]. Just imagine what might have happened to human populations if there were an eruption ten times larger than Tambora. That might have been what happened 73,500 years ago when the Toba "supereruption" exploded just as humans were moving out of Africa and colonizing the rest of the world.[9] The Toba volcano, which is located on the island of Sumatra in Indonesia, exploded with a VEI of 8, the largest known eruption on earth. The resulting plumes of volcanic ash and sulfur aerosols drastically reduced the amount of solar radiation reaching the earth after the explosion. The aerosol plumes slowly dispersed over the next ten years, but not until the earth's average temperature decreased by as much as 3°C to 5°C. These cold temperatures, which seem to have lasted for up to 1,000 years, are clearly recorded in the $\delta^{18}O$ record in Greenland ice cores (Figure 12.1).

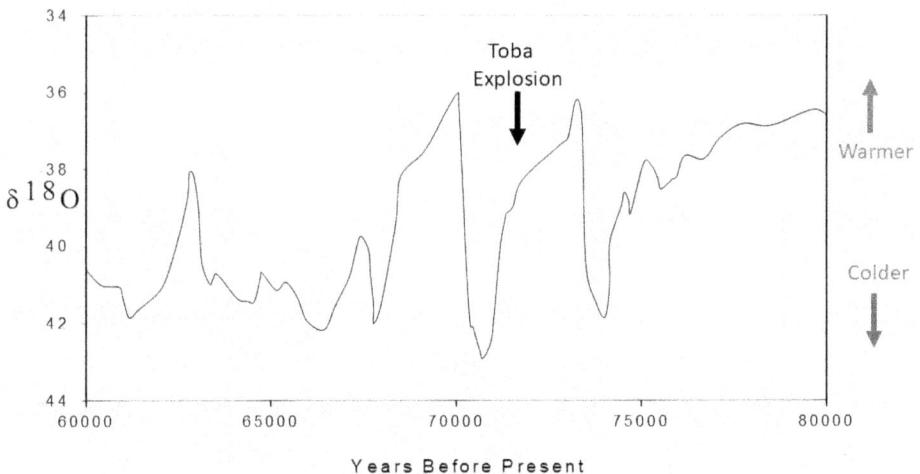

Figure 12.1. The $\delta^{18}O$ record of the GISP2 ice core (Greenland) for the period between 60,000 and 80,000 years ago showing the cooling trend that started after the Toba explosion. Data is from Rapino and Ambrose (2000)[9].

The effects of such cold temperatures on vegetation, particularly vegetation in tropical areas not acclimated to colder conditions, must have been devastating. With a serious depletion of vegetation, many different creatures, including humans, would have come under stress. Those stresses may have led to the pre-60,000 "bottleneck" that drastically reduced human populations around the world in the late Pleistocene.[9,10,11]

But beginning about 50,000 years ago, human populations apparently recovered and began expanding rapidly. This expansion may reflect some genetic changes induced by the stress of the bottleneck, resulting in increased human cognitive abilities. Alternatively, or perhaps in addition, it might reflect technological advances made after 50,000 years ago that increased human rates of survival. In any case, one outcome of the human population bottleneck is that all modern humans are characterized by remarkable genetic homogeneity. Yes, there have been genetic changes characteristic to isolated populations such as Europeans, Asians, and Africans that are reflected in mtDNA.[11] Nevertheless, all modern humans have a much higher degree of genetic similarity than almost any other mammalian species.

Whether or not the eruption of Tambora affected the Battle of Waterloo, or whether the supereruption of Toba caused the human genetic bottleneck is not really the point. The point is that volcanic eruptions can be a major instigator of climate reversals that can, in less than a year, produce profound global cooling. The aftermath of the Tambora eruption of 1815 also shows that such cooling can cause a great deal of human misery in the form of famine and epidemics. Finally, the effects of volcanic eruptions can interact with other processes such as sunspot minimums. The Dalton Minimum of 1790-1830 almost certainly exacerbated the cooling that followed Tambora. Alternatively, it's also likely that normal or enhanced sunspot formation could ameliorate volcano-triggered cooling.

As with anything having to do with climate change, it's never just one thing.

REFERENCES

1. Oppenheimer, C., 2012. Eruptions that shook the world. Cambridge University Press 392 p.

2. Genge, M.J., 2018. Electrostatic levitation of volcanic ash into the ionosphere and its abrupt effect on climate. Geology, 46(10), pp.835-838.

3. Klingaman, W.K. and Klingaman, N.P., 2013. The year without summer: 1816 and the volcano that darkened the world and changed history. St. Martin's Press, New York, NY, 338 p.

4. Cao, S., Li, Y. and Yang, B., 2012. Mt. Tambora, climatic changes, and China's decline in the nineteenth century. Journal of World History, pp.587-607.

5. Guevara-Murua, A., Williams, C.A., Hendy, E.J., Rust, A.C. and Cashman, K.V., 2014. Observations of a stratospheric aerosol veil from a tropical volcanic eruption in December 1808: is this the Unknown~ 1809 eruption?
Climate of the Past, 10(5), pp.1707-1722.

6. Cole, P.D., Robertson, R.E.A., Fedele, L. and Scarpati, C., 2019. Explosive activity of the last 1000 years at La Soufrière, St Vincent, Lesser Antilles. Journal of Volcanology and Geothermal Research, 371, pp.86-100.

7. William G. Atkins, History of Hawley (West Cummington, Mass.) (1887), p, 86.

8. Oppenheimer, C., 2003. Climatic, environmental and human consequences of the largest known historic eruption: Tambora volcano (Indonesia) 1815. Progress in physical geography, 27(2), pp.230-259.

9. Rampino, M.R. and Ambrose, S.H., 2000. Volcanic winter in the Garden of Eden: the Toba supereruption and the late Pleistocene human population crash. Special Papers-Geological Society of Americapp.71-82.

10. Cann, R.L., Stoneking, M. and Wilson, A.C., 1987. Mitochondrial DNA and human evolution. Nature, 325(6099), pp.31-36.

11. Harpending, H.C., Sherry, S.T., Rogers, A.R. and Stoneking, M., 1993. The genetic structure of ancient human populations. Current Anthropology, 34(4), pp.483-496.

CHAPTER 13

Krakatoa and the Development of the Atmospheric and Geologic Sciences

IN THE MORNING OF JANUARY 20, 1884, Joseph Wharton left his house, about six miles north of Philadelphia's city center, in the middle of a snowstorm. Wharton, one of the founders of Bethlehem Steel and the future founder of the University of Pennsylvania's Wharton School, was on a mission to solve an atmospheric puzzle. Throughout the fall and winter of 1883, the sunrises and sunsets had been unusually colorful. These "splendid roseate glows" had been noticed all over the world, and in Wharton's words:[1]

> *gave rise to many conjectures, but apparently to almost no experiments. A few persons believed those glows to be sunlight reflected from the under surface of a stratum of fine solid particles suspended at a great height in the atmosphere; some thought with me that those particles might be volcanic dust which had floated to us from the eruption at Krakatoa, but, as no one offered any proof of this, I attempted on the morning of January 20, 1884, to demonstrate it.*

Wharton, noticing that the snow was falling in a "calm atmosphere, presumably from a high altitude," wondered if it might contain evidence of any "fine solid particles."

Accordingly, Wharton carried a large porcelain bowl to an open field near his house and collected about a gallon of the newly fallen snow. He covered the bowl, took it to his house, and let the snow melt. At first, he did not detect any "sediment." But by gently swirling the bowl, concentrating any solids in the deepest part, he poured off the excess water and let the rest evaporate. When it had dried, he could distinguish "a minute quantity of fine dust discerned by the tiny vitreous reflections it gave in the sunlight." Putting some of the "dust" under his microscope, he observed that:

> *it consisted in part of irregular, flattish, blobby fragments, mostly transparent and showing no trace of crystalline structure, in part of transparent filaments more or less contorted, sometimes attached together in wisps, and most sprinkled with minute glass particles. The filaments of glass had about the same diameter as single filaments of silk placed on the microscope slide for comparison with them.*

Because of his experience at Bethlehem Steel, Wharton was a capable mineralogist. Judging the quality of various iron ores, as well as identifying associated non-iron bearing minerals that might lower its value, was an important part of his business. In particular, he immediately noticed that the particles were "showing no trace of crystalline structures." Most natural rocks, he knew, are composed entirely of crystalline minerals. Since the snow-derived particles seemed to be non-crystalline and glass-like, it deepened his suspicion that these particles might be of volcanic origin.

But it didn't prove it. In fact, the particles may have come from his own nearby smelting furnaces which belched smoke and ash when in use. Accordingly, he obtained "dust" samples from the Bethlehem steel works and examined them under the microscope as well. The steel works particles were "largely spheroidal or globular, with a few filaments." They clearly differed from the snow-derived particles.

At this point, living near the port of Philadelphia gave Wharton another avenue of inquiry. In early February, a ship named the J.E. Ridgeway arrived at Philadelphia from the Island of Manila by way of the Strait of Sunda. That is where the Krakatoa eruption had taken place beginning in May of 1883 before reaching its catastrophic climax on August 27, 1883. Wharton visited the ship and discovered from the ship's log that it had encountered a vast field of floating pumice about five hundred miles from the eruption site. One of the ship's mates had collected some samples of the pumice and gave a few grams to Wharton. Taking the pumice samples back to his microscope, he "recognized just such transparent flattish scraps and ragged accretions as were present among the dust found in the snow-fall of January 20." Wharton concluded his paper, read before the American Philosophical Society in 1884, as follows:

> *It is difficult to resist the conclusions (1) that the vitreous dust found in the snow-fall of January 20, 1884, was not derived from iron or steel furnaces, (2) that it was of similar origin to the floating pumice found by the ship J. E. Ridgeway, (3) that it was ejected by the huge volcanic explosions of Krakatoa.*

Wharton was not alone in wondering about the effects of the Krakatoa eruption on the earth's atmosphere. The Tambora eruption of 1815 became known in Europe and America several months after it happened. That amount of time was typical for information to travel around the world in the days of sailing ships. But by 1883, telegraph lines had been laid around much of the world, and news of the May eruption of Krakatoa reached London within a few days. At first, the story was considered barely newsworthy and was mentioned only by a single newspaper.[2] As the summer continued, however, and particularly after news of the August 27 catastrophic explosions became known,

Krakatoa became a very big story. Like Joseph Wharton, dozens of scientists around the world took note, and it initiated a revolution in both the geologic and atmospheric sciences.

⟺

The August 27 eruption of Krakatoa, which featured as many as four violent explosions, was a cataclysmic disaster. It wasn't so much of a disaster for the humans living near the volcano because the island of Krakatoa was uninhabited. Furthermore, anybody living near it could plainly see that something bad was about to happen. Erupting volcanos were nothing new to the Javanese and Sumatrans, and no doubt there was a rich oral history concerning eruptions in the past. Most people living anywhere near Krakatoa simply moved away. The disaster was caused by the explosions, the associated pyroclastic flows of pumice and lava, and by the final collapse of the volcanic caldera. Each of those events generated huge tsunamis, some estimated to be more than one-hundred-feet high that pummeled the surrounding islands.

Alexander Patrick Cameron, the British consul at the city of Batavia (now called Jakarta) on the island of Java one hundred miles from Krakatoa, provided a written report a few days after the explosive conflagration. He vividly described the destruction wrought by the tsunamis:

> *The destruction caused by the waves on shore both to life and property (is) known from reports already to hand to be very widespread....the whole of the southeastern coast of Sumatra must have suffered severely from the effects of the sudden influx of the sea, and thousands of natives inhabiting the villages on the coast must have almost certainly perished.*

Perish they did. The best estimates of the fatalities caused by the eruption and the resulting tsunamis are in excess of 36,000 souls. The scale of the eruption and its aftermath captured the world's imagination. Soon after the eruption, the blazing red sunrises and sunsets—which were quickly and correctly attributed to the eruption—only intensified that interest. Within a few months, dozens of amateur scientists (such as John Wharton and his snow-melting experiments), as well as professional scientists, began looking into various aspects of the eruption and its atmospheric effects.

Of particular interest to many people were the startlingly colorful sunsets and sunrises. At first, many people were skeptical that volcanic dust could be transported to and maintained in suspension in the upper atmosphere for months or years. It was thought that the air would simply be too thin, but there was no doubt that the colorful phenomena were real. As early as 1884, a German scientist named Georg Neumayer used geographical reports and logbooks to show that the phenomenal sunsets were connected with the Krakatoa eruption.[3] But the physics and chemistry causing the unusual sunsets were still a mystery.

Another German named Johann Kiessling, a teacher at a prestigious science school in Hamburg, also studied the "sunset" phenomena. Earlier in 1868, an Irish physicist named John Tyndall had invented an experimental apparatus for forming clouds in a glass tube.[4] Kiessling built a similar apparatus with a glass sphere to reproduce the colorful effects seen at sunset. One of those effects was "Bishops rings," a diffuse brown or bluish halo observed around the sun. This phenomenon was first observed after the August 27 eruption of Krakatoa by a clergyman named Rev. Sereno Edwards, Bishop of Honolulu. Working with his apparatus, Kiessling showed that the colored Bishops rings could not be explained solely by the reflection or absorption of light, but instead required a component of refraction, splitting white light into its colorful rainbow components.

In addition, experiments conducted by Kiessler and the physicist Hermann von Helmholtz demonstrated that sulfuric acid aerosols greatly enhanced cloud and fog formation.[4] They were investigating sulfuric acid because in June 1783, the eruption of an Icelandic volcano named Laki had caused a widespread and persistent haze over most of Europe. In addition, several observers of the haze noticed a distinct sulfuric smell in connection with the haze.[4] Kiessler's and Helmholtz's experiments confirmed the importance of sulfuric acid aerosols in atmospheric chemistry. The central role that volcanic sulfur aerosols play in affecting the earth's climate wasn't fully appreciated until later in the twentieth century.[5] The more important point is that, as horrendous as the eruption was for the Indonesians, the Krakatoa eruption contributed a great deal to the development of experimental atmospheric science in both Europe and America.

Something similar happened with the practice of geology as well. By the time of the Krakatoa eruption, nineteenth-century geology simply had no explanation for what caused volcanic eruptions. For the ancient Greeks, who often witnessed volcanic eruptions, it seemed obvious there was fire inside the Earth. Anaxagoras of Clazomenae (510-428 BCE) said as much when he noted the thick clouds of vapor that rose up with great violence. He also suggested volcanos were the source of earthquakes. Aristotle (384-322 BCE) largely agreed that volcanos had to be caused by fires within the earth. In his *Meteorologica* he wrote, "The earth possesses its own internal fire," which in turn produced "winds" in the subsurface. When those superheated winds periodically escaped violently from the subsurface, volcanos resulted.

The Romans initially accepted the Greek theories of fire and winds in the earth as the cause of volcanos. But Seneca (2 BCE-65 CE) extended that idea by proposing that friction created by circulating air ignited flammable rocks within the earth:

*Now it is obvious that underground there are large
quantities of sulfur and other substances no less
inflammable. When the air in search of a path of escape
works its tortuous way through ground of this nature, it
necessarily kindles fire by mere friction.*

The idea of fire inside the earth persisted throughout the Middle
Ages right up to the modern era. The Italian Jesuit priest Athanasius
Kircher (1602-1680) went so far as to have himself lowered by a rope
into the crater of Mount Vesuvius, which was spewing gaseous vapors
and about to erupt. In his book *Mundus Subterraneus* (The Subterra-
nean World, 1664), he postulated that the caverns underlying the earth
were partly filled with fires and that volcanos and their accompanying
earthquakes were the result.

Rene Descartes (1596-1650) devised a different idea for the origin
of the heat clearly present within the earth. Descartes thought that the
earth had originated much like our sun, the only difference being that
the earth was smaller. In other words, the earth had begun as a molten
mass (a star?) that cooled over time. As it cooled, the denser material
gravitated to the center of the earth and remained molten because of the
incandescent properties of the former star. That core was surrounded
by an intermediate layer that had solidified as the planet cooled. That
layer, in turn, was surrounded by the solid crust we see at land surface. That three-layer model for the earth's interior structure was very
influential and suggested that the earth's molten center stored a prime-
val source of heat that periodically forced its way to land surface and
caused volcanos to erupt.

By 1883, Descartes' explanation for volcanos was the state of the
art in volcanology. The eruption of Krakatoa, however, altered that.
As it happens, a Dutch geologist named Rogier D.M. Verbeek had
made a preliminary visit to Krakatoa in 1880. That visit seems to have

piqued Verbeek's curiosity because after the first small eruptions in May of 1883, one of his assistants revisited the island to collect ash and lava samples from the Perbuwatan vent, one of three vents on the island. Later chemical analysis of those samples showed that a dark-colored ash at the base of the vent had a silica content of 51%, while the overlying whitish ash had a silica content of more than 65%. It was almost as if the volcano were erupting two distinct kinds of lava and ash. That observation's significance, however, wouldn't be understood for another hundred years. At the beginning of the eruption, the magma chamber underlying the volcano was filled with a stiff high-silica magma that was actually plugging the three vents. But when a hot, viscous, low-silica basaltic lava was injected into the magma chamber, it seems to have provided the spark that initiated the explosions.[6] The two different kinds of magma explains the two kinds of ash.

Verbeek happened to be on a ship that steamed past Krakatoa in July of 1883, and so he witnessed some of the eruption. When the final explosions occurred in August, Verbeek heard them at home in Batavia a hundred miles away. In the chaotic aftermath of the explosion and the accompanying tsunamis, Verbeek was sent to gather information and to report to the Dutch government as to how it should respond. Verbeek spent a year and a half on the task. His 495-page report published in 1885 contains detailed observations on the eruptions, the chemical composition of the ash and lava, the sounds of the explosions, and the resulting tsunamis.[7]

Several of Verbeek's conclusions have, in retrospect, been confirmed over the years. For example, Verbeek believed that the destructive tsunamis were not generated directly by the explosions, but rather by the pyroclastic flows that raced down the vents, hit the ocean at a high velocity, and displaced huge volumes of seawater. Similarly, the distinctive sounds of the "explosions" probably were generated by pyroclastic flows striking the water. He estimated that the ash plume reached between fifteen and twenty kilometers in height, which in retrospect was an underestimate. He correctly surmised that the colorful sunsets and sunrises were caused by ash and aerosol injected into the upper atmosphere. Finally, by corresponding with a colleague in Spain, he confirmed that the eruption's ash particles could be found in melted snow, just as Joseph Wharton in Pennsylvania had concluded.

The Krakatoa eruption, a disaster for Indonesia resulting in several years of cooler global weather, ironically was not a disaster for everyone. Most of the climate reversals we've talked about in this book have meant bad news for agriculture and human populations. The cooling climate at the end of the Roman Warm Period was such an example, with crop failure followed by famines and epidemics. Those effects, in turn, contributed to the mass migrations of people desperately trying to find land and food. The cooler weather that prevailed for three or four years after the Krakatoa explosion *was* bad news for some people, but for the people living in southern Spain, the cooler weather turned out to be good news.

The cause of the cooler weather was, of course, the scattering of incoming shortwave solar radiation by sulfur aerosols injected into the stratosphere by the erupting volcano. In addition, less solar radiation reached land surface. We know this happened in the south of Spain in the years following the Krakatoa eruption because of an astronomical instrument installed at the San Fernando Observatory in 1881. The instrument, called a Campbell-Stokes sunshine recorder, consisted of a solid glass sphere that concentrates the sun's rays to a point on a strip of calibrated paper, burning it. The intensity and position of the burn indicates the time and intensity of the sunshine during daylight hours. The records from before and after the 1883 eruption show a marked decrease in sunshine intensity beginning in 1883, reaching a minimum value in 1884. The decrease in sunshine intensity lasted at least to 1887, and this is the earliest demonstration that volcanic explosions can decrease the amount of solar radiation reaching the earth.[8]

One might assume a decrease in solar radiation would be bad news for agriculture. That assumption would be true for higher latitudes, but southern Spain has a climate unlike the rest of Europe. Specifically, its climate is arid for much of the year (summer) with torrential rains occurring periodically (generally in winter or spring). This part of Spain, therefore, experiences both prolonged droughts that then give way to occasional floods, a very challenging climate for grain agriculture.

In the years following the Krakatoa explosion, however, southern Spain experienced a significant decrease in maximum temperatures, an increase in minimum temperatures, and an increase in rainfall. The increased rainfall was more evenly spaced, and for several years after the eruption, fewer floods occurred. The net socioeconomic impact of the Krakatoa event on southern Spain's agriculture was an *increase* in grain harvests and a *decrease* in grain prices.[9] Salvador Gil-Guirado, the lead author of the paper that reported these happy results, gave it the playful title *The blessing of the 'year without summer': Climatic and socioeconomic impact of the Krakatoa eruption (1883) in the south-east of the Iberian Peninsula.*

It's an example of how climate reversals are not always bad, at least for some people.

REFERENCES

1. Wharton, J., 1894. Dust from the Krakatoa Eruption of 1883. Proceedings of the American Philosophical Society, 32(143), pp.343-345.

2. Winchester, S. 2003. Krakatoa: The Day the World Exploded, August 27, 1883. Harper Collins, New York, New York. 416 pp.

3. Schröder, W. and Wiederkehr, K.H., 2000. Johann Kiessling, the Krakatoa event and the development of atmosheric optics after 1883. Notes and Records of the Royal Society of London, 54(2), pp.249-258.

4. Malila, J., 2018. On the early studies recognizing the role of sulphuric acid in atmospheric haze and new particle formation. Tellus B: Chemical and Physical Meteorology, 70(1), pp.1-11.

5. Thordarson, T. and Self, S., 2003. Atmospheric and environmental effects of the 1783–1784 Laki eruption: A review and reassessment. Journal of Geophysical Research: Atmospheres, 108(D1), pp.AAC-7.

6. Self, S., 1992. Krakatau revisited: the course of events and interpretation of the 1883 eruption. GeoJournal, 28(2), pp.109-121.

7. Verbeek, R.D.M. 1885. Krakatau. Government Press, Batavia. 495 pp.

8. Obregón, M.A., Gallego, M.C., Antón, M. and Vaquero, J.M., 2020. Sunshine duration data in San Fernando (South of Spain) during 1880s: The impact of Krakatoa volcanic eruption. Geoscience Data Journal, 7(2), pp.185-191.

9. Gil-Guirado, S., Olcina-Cantos, J. and Pérez-Morales, A., 2021. The blessing of the "year without summer": Climatic and socioeconomic impact of the Krakatoa eruption (1883) in the south-east of the Iberian Peninsula. International Journal of Climatology, 41(4), pp.2279-2300.

CHAPTER 14

The Mount Pinatubo Eruption of 1991: A Modern Climate Reversal

IN 1997, THE MINNESOTA DEPARTMENT of Natural Resources (MDNR) began receiving complaints from some fishermen that their walleye catches had decreased noticeably. Walleye are one of the more popular gamefish that inhabit Minnesota's more than 10,000 lakes. More specifically, the fishermen were suspicious that for budgetary reasons the MDNR had reduced the numbers of walleye fry and fingerlings stocked annually in particular lakes. An MDNR biologist named Dennis Schupp examined the matter.[1] His investigation took several years, and he systematically considered possible reasons for the lower walleye population.

In response to the charge that MDNR had reduced walleye fingerling stocking, Schupp documented the yearly numbers of walleye fingerlings and fry stocked between 1979 and 1997. While the numbers varied from year to year, they remained in the range of several million fingerlings and several hundred million fry per year. It didn't look like stocking rates could explain the lower catches. Secondly, the number of walleye catches in lakes that practiced gill netting, a useful proxy for walleye abundance, was also documented. Curiously, Schupp found that the catch numbers generally *increased* between 1979 and 1997. The catch numbers, however, decreased in 1998. What could have caused the declines?

To answer that question, Schupp looked at mean air temperatures in Minnesota for the spring and summer from 1979 through 1997. As it happens, air temperatures in the spring are critical for the hatch rate and survival of walleye fry. Colder temperatures depress survival rates while warmer temperatures enhance them. The generally increasing temperatures between 1979 and 1997 (global warming during the Modern Warm Time) certainly contributed to the observed trend of increasing walleye catches during that period. However, there was a marked decrease in Minnesota spring air temperatures for 1992 and 1993. During those two years, spring air temperatures were 3.3°C cooler than the years immediately before and after. Because female walleye mature sexually in five years, a decreased fry survival rate in 1992-1993 would show up as decreased catches in 1998. Running the statistics, Schupp calculated that those colder spring temperatures could explain up to 58% of the observed decrease in walleye catches.

But Schupp took one more step. He knew that Mt Pinatubo on the Island of Luzon in the Philippine Islands had erupted violently on June 15, 1991. He also knew that the plume of sulfur aerosols that had been blown into the stratosphere had cooled global temperatures by 1°C between 1992 and 1993. Schupp asked the simple question "What does Mt Pinatubo have to do with walleyes?" in a paper published in 2002.[1]

⟺

Thus far, the climate reversals we've considered—the ends of the Late Bronze Age, the Roman Warm Period, and the Medieval Warm Period being examples—are attested to by contemporary textual evidence, geochemical evidence from ice cores and deep-sea sediment cores, as well as biological evidence such as tree rings and plant pollen. But those events happened prior to the development of the modern earth and climate sciences. That changed, however, with the eruption of Mt Pinatubo. Here was a reasonably large volcanic event with a volcanic explosive index of six (VEI-6) that could be observed and studied with a full range of geologic and climatic tools, as well as with satellite-based sensors. These tools and sensors have greatly increased our understanding of the physics, chemistry, and biology associated with volcanic events and the climate reversals that they can trigger.

In October of 1984, the space shuttle *Challenger* was launched from Cape Kennedy on its sixth mission into earth's orbit. Unhappily, the *Challenger* is more often remembered for its tenth mission which ended in its disintegration seventy-three seconds into the launch. But on that day in 1984, everything went smoothly, and *Challenger* reached orbit eight and a half minutes after launch. Later that day, the crew attempted to deploy the Earth Radiation Budget Satellite (ERBS), one of the principal goals of the shuttle mission. Immediately after deployment, however, one of the ERBS's solar panels failed to extend properly, raising the possibility that the deployment would fail. Mission specialist Sally Ride was able to extend the shuttle's remotely controlled robotic arm, grab ahold of the stuck panel, and maneuver it into the sunlight, allowing the panel to extend properly. The ERBS has the distinction of being the first satellite to be successfully deployed from a space shuttle.

The successful deployment and operation of the ERBS was a giant step forward for the atmospheric and climate sciences. One of the instruments carried by ERBS, called the Stratospheric Aerosol and Gas Experiment (SAGE II), was originally intended to monitor the spatial and temporal distribution of tropospheric aerosols such as dust from the Saharan and Saudi Arabian deserts, haze from industrialized urban areas, and smoke from forest fires and agricultural burning. In June of 1991, however, the satellite was serendipitously in place to monitor the development and fate of Mt Pinatubo's volcanic ash and aerosol plume as it was blown up into the atmosphere.[2]

Following the Mt Pinatubo eruption, an evolving plume of ash, water vapor, and sulfurous gases was transported upward into the stratosphere and moved westwards, circling the globe in twenty-one days. A variety of instrumentation monitored the plume, including ground- and aircraft-based LIDAR (Light Detection and Ranging), solar photometers, balloon-borne and aircraft-borne aerosol counters, as well as the satellite-borne instruments of the ERBS.[3] The total mass of sulfur oxides (SO_2) injected into the atmosphere was estimated to be 20 teragrams, or about 44 trillion pounds. This SO_2 began a series of chemical reactions that converted it into sulfuric acid and ice ($H_2SO_4/$ H_2O) aerosols. An aerosol, incidentally, is a suspension of fine solid or liquid particles in air such as dust, fog, or fine particles of sulfuric acid generated by volcanos.

The aircraft and ground-based LIDAR measurements indicated that most of the aerosols produced by Mt Pinatubo were concentrated in the stratosphere at altitudes ranging from 21 to 27 kilometers. In addition, the development, dispersion, and dissipation of the aerosol plume from the Mt Pinatubo eruption was monitored by the SAGE II sensor over a two-year period.[3] The longitudinal movement of the plume initially tracked westward along the equator before gradually spreading out over much of the planet. There was an immediate two order of magnitude increase in optical depth imparted by the sulfur aerosols following the eruption, and effects continued for two years following the eruption until finally dispersing.

It had been observed, going back at least to the 1815 eruption of Mt Tambora and the 1883 eruption of Krakatoa, that the sun becomes partially obscured by the plume of volcanic particles and gases in the stratosphere. Scientists had long suspected that the reflection of some of the sun's incoming radiation out into space could contribute to that effect. They also expected that that process could lead to atmospheric cooling. The 1991 eruption of Mt Pinatubo provided an opportunity to test those hypotheses.

The earth's albedo (the capacity to reflect solar radiation out into space) was also monitored by the ERBS satellite. This data provided the first unambiguous evidence that the earth's albedo in the summer of 1991 did, in fact, increase significantly and was much higher than the average for the preceding five years.[4] In cloud-free regions of the earth, which normally have a low albedo, albedo increased by 20% due to light-scattering by the aerosol plume.

Those results certainly imply that the solar radiation reaching the earth's surface should decrease. Another sensor carried by the ERBS, a wide-field-of-view radiometer, made it possible to directly measure both the amount of short-wave radiation coming from the sun and how much of it is scattered into space by the earth's atmosphere. That detector also measured the long-wave infrared (heat) radiation generated by short-wave solar radiation reaching earth's surface. The long-wave radiation is important to the heat budget of the earth because it is absorbed by the greenhouse gases, which store heat in the atmosphere (Fig. 1.3).

The Mt Pinatubo eruption happened during a time when the earth's atmosphere was experiencing a warming trend. But despite that overall warming trend, global temperatures actually dropped in 1992 and 1993 (Figure 14.1) before resuming the overall warming trend. While the Mt Pinatubo technically qualifies as a climate reversal, it was certainly a rather mild one.

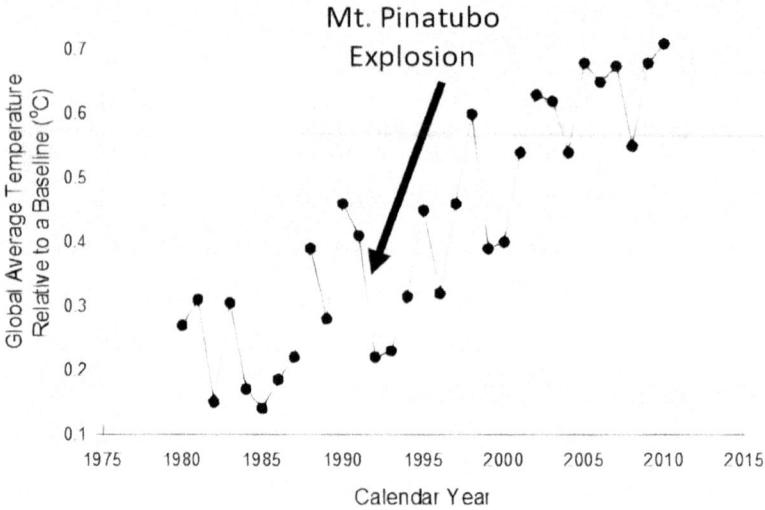

Figure 14.1. Graph showing the general warming trend between 1980 and 2010 that was interrupted by the Mt Pinatubo eruption in 1991 and 1992 before resuming the warming trend in 1995.

The Mt Pinatubo eruption also shed some light on one of the most important, and contentious, issues in climate science: how the greenhouse gases carbon dioxide and water vapor interact to influence episodes of atmospheric warming and cooling. Radiation coming from the sun is predominantly of the short-wave variety, with wavelengths ranging from 0.01 to 0.4 micrometers (μm). When short-wave radiation hits the earth's surface, it produces heat. That heat is then emitted as long-wave infrared radiation with wavelengths ranging from 0.78 to 1,000 μm. This long-wave radiation is then radiated into the atmosphere and ultimately back into space (Fig. 1.3). This is where the greenhouse gases enter the story. Water vapor absorbs long-wave radiation at several wavelengths between 1.0 and 70 μm, effectively trapping some of the heat in the atmosphere. Similarly, CO_2 absorbs long-wave radiation at several wavelengths between 2 and 11 μm, trapping more thermal energy in the atmosphere. It's been estimated that without greenhouse gases, the earth's mean surface temperature would be about 0°F. With the greenhouse gases presently in the atmosphere (predominantly water vapor and CO_2), the mean surface temperature of the earth is about 15°C. Clearly we wouldn't want to do without greenhouse gases in the earth's atmosphere.

But here comes the rub. The amount of water vapor the atmosphere can hold is hugely temperature dependent. Really cold air can contain as little as 0.01% water vapor, whereas warm air can hold as much as 3%. Furthermore, the residence time of water vapor in the atmosphere is just on the order of a few days. The residence time of CO_2, on the other hand, can be several hundred years. If the atmosphere warms due to increasing concentrations of CO_2, that warming could increase the water vapor content of the atmosphere, magnifying the warming effects of the CO_2. Climate scientists call this the *water vapor feedback* effect.

Alternatively, one might think that as a warming atmosphere increases its water vapor content, the earth's cloud cover might increase as well. Since clouds reflect short-wave solar radiation into space, it's possible that increased water vapor content could lead to a cooler atmosphere. Furthermore, since these processes interact, one can easily imagine that water vapor feedback could lead to increased warming, increased cooling, or something in between. One can see why the water vapor feedback effect is so important and so contentious. Does it increase or decrease CO_2-driven global warming?

The Mt Pinatubo eruption was a naturally occurring phenomenon that measurably impacted the earth's climate (Fig. 14.1), including both the atmosphere's temperature and its water vapor content, raising the possibility that the Mt Pinatubo perturbations can be treated as a natural experiment for observing the water vapor feedback effect. In their 2002 paper, Brian Soden and his colleagues at NOAA, Princeton University, and Rutgers University used satellite-based data to document that the Pinatubo aerosol plume decreased the amount of short-wave radiation from the sun reaching the earth's surface.[5] Satellite-derived data also showed a corresponding decrease in long-wave infrared radiation emanating from the earth back towards space. These effects were accompanied by a drop in atmospheric temperatures and water vapor concentrations, also based on satellite measurements.

From a qualitative point of view, these observed changes are entirely consistent with the water vapor feedback effect. Soden and colleagues then compared the satellite observations with the results of an atmospheric general circulation model (GCM) to tease out how much of the changes could be attributed to water vapor feedback. They found that by removing the water vapor feedback effect, the model underestimated the observed temperature decline by about 30%. They concluded that the atmospheric perturbations caused by the Mt Pinatubo eruption provided a real-world demonstration of how the water vapor feedback effect could affect global temperatures.

Soden and colleagues present a compelling story, and one that may well be close to the truth. But in the spirit of healthy skepticism, two points bear consideration. First, and as Soden and his colleagues themselves point out, the Mt Pinatubo climate perturbation was a temperature *decrease*. How applicable those results might be to a temperature *increase* due to CO_2-driven global warming is not particularly clear. Secondly, the team used "an atmospheric GCM with *specified clouds* coupled to a mixed-layer ocean...".[5] In other words, it seems that while water vapor feedback in the GCM was varied, cloud cover was not. Because cloud cover is an essential variable determining how much short-wave radiation reaches the earth's surface (Fig. 1.3) and because water vapor feedback almost certainly affects cloud formation, it raises questions about the modeled temperature forecasts.

⇔

The Krakatoa eruption of 1883 happened at a time when widespread almost instantaneous communications (telegraph) were available. It also happened at a time when the atmospheric and earth sciences had developed to the point that people could begin to understand how and why such eruptions could affect the earth's climate (chapter 13). Similarly, the Mt Pinatubo eruption (1991) happened only a few years after climate- and radiation-monitoring satellites were in place and were capable of measuring how much radiation was reaching the earth before and after the eruption. The eruptions of Krakatoa and Pinatubo, especially Krakatoa, were terrible disasters for the people of Indonesia and the Philippines respectively. It is a dark irony, however, that those eruptions have provided so much insight into how the earth works (volcanos) and why the earth's climate has always experienced alternate episodes of warming and cooling.

REFERENCES

1. Schupp, D.H., 2002. What does Mt. Pinatubo have to do with walleyes? North American Journal of Fisheries Management, 22(3), pp.1014-1020.

2. McCormick, M. and Veiga, R.E., 1992. SAGE II measurements of early Pinatubo aerosols. Geophysical Research Letters, 19(2), pp.155-158.

3. McCormick, M.P., Thomason, L.W. and Trepte, C.R., 1995. Atmospheric effects of the Mt Pinatubo eruption. Nature, 373(6513), pp.399-404.

4. Minnis, P., Harrison, E.F., Stowe, L.L., Gibson, G.G., Denn, F.M., Doelling, D.R. and Smith, W.L., 1993. Radiative climate forcing by the Mount Pinatubo eruption. Science, 259(5100), pp.1411-1415.

5. Soden, B.J., Wetherald, R.T., Stenchikov, G.L. and Robock, A., 2002. Global cooling after the eruption of Mount Pinatubo: A test of climate feedback by water vapor. Science, 296(5568), pp.727-730.

EPILOGUE
Dealing with Climate Reversals

THE EARTH'S CLIMATE SYSTEM is a marvel of happenstance, thermody-namic balance, and the benevolent influence of living organisms.[1] Of those three, happenstance—the fortuitous position of the earth in rela-tion to the sun—is the most important. The average distance between the earth and the sun is ninety-four million miles, and the earth's aver-age surface temperature is 15°C. Venus, on the other hand is only sixty-seven million miles from the sun, and its average surface temperature is 464° C. Venus's higher temperature is partly because of its relative proximity to the sun and partly because its atmosphere is 96.5% car-bon dioxide, a powerful greenhouse gas. Mars, on the other hand is located 131 million miles from the sun, has practically no atmosphere at all, and has an average surface temperature of -60°C. Clearly, earth's fortuitous position relative to the sun, as well as the composition of its atmosphere (78% nitrogen, 21% oxygen, 0.0407% carbon dioxide), provides temperatures that are amenable to water-based life.

Also under the heading of happenstance is the fact that earth has an intrinsic magnetic field provided by its liquid-iron core and its rotation. Both Mars and Venus lack an intrinsic magnetic field. In the case of Mars, it clearly did have liquid water on its surface sometime after it coalesced four or five billion years ago. But since Mars lacks a magnetic field, the solar wind swept that water out into space long ago. Venus, because of its proximity to the sun, does have a weak magnetic field induced by the solar wind. However, the runaway greenhouse effect conferred by its carbon dioxide atmosphere precludes the presence of water-based life, at least on the planet's surface.

There are many components of the earth's thermodynamic balance, the most obvious of which is the earth's rate of rotation. Because earth completely rotates once every twenty-four hours, incoming solar radiation is dispersed relatively evenly around the planet. A substantially slower rotation would increase the temperature contrast between night and day. A faster rate of rotation would decrease the temperature contrast. Whatever that contrast happens to be, it feeds the wind circulation patterns that spread heat around the globe. Those same heat contrasts, along with contrasts in ocean salinity, drive the ocean currents that also distribute heat around the world.

That leaves the effects that living organisms, animals and plants, have on the climate. Animals, along with the hundreds of volcanos presently active on the earth, produce carbon dioxide which serves to trap heat in the atmosphere. Plants, on the other hand, consume carbon dioxide and combine it with water to manufacture sugars, releasing gaseous oxygen into the atmosphere. The balance between carbon dioxide production and consumption, and thus the temperature of the atmosphere, has varied widely over geologic time. When carbon dioxide consumption outpaces production, the planet's atmosphere cools. That has happened several times in the last two billion years resulting in what geologists call a "snowball earth." Conversely when carbon dioxide production exceeds consumption, the earth's atmosphere warms, as happened most recently in the time of the dinosaurs sixty million years ago.

In the 6,000 years of written human history, there have been at least five major warm-to-cool climate reversals. These occurred at the end of the Late Bronze age (1200 BCE), the beginning of the Late Antique

Little Ice Age (400 CE), the beginning of the first Little Ice Age (1300 CE), the second Little Ice Age (1600 CE), and the third Little Ice Age (1815 CE) (Figure 10.1). That historical record suggests one climate reversal every 1,200 years or so. Curiously enough, that roughly agrees with the six periodic ice-rafting events in the North Atlantic Ocean going back 10,000 years (Figure 10.2). So, can we expect a warm-to-cold climate reversal every 1,000 to 2,000 years?

Probably not.

The problem with that sort of thinking is the fact that many recorded warm-to-cold climate reversals were associated with explosive volcanic events, and the timing of such events is completely unpredictable. What we can conclude, however, is that the earth's climate has never been constant. It is continually changing in response to multiple processes that interact with each other in ways that we don't, and probably never will, fully understand. One hundred fifty years ago the earth entered a warming trend that ended the Little Ice Age that had extended from 1300 to 1860 CE. This warming trend reflects several things that have increased the amount of solar radiation reaching the earth's surface. One of those things is that the earth's orbit is presently nearly circular, which keeps the earth nearer to the sun and increases the amount of solar radiation reaching the earth. Also, the fact that the North Pole is tilted toward the sun during the winter increases average winter temperatures in the northern hemisphere. That probably is one reason the most recent ice age began to end 15,000 years ago. The modern warming trend also reflects the rapid increase in atmospheric carbon dioxide concentrations in the atmosphere due to fossil fuel combustion.

The present global warming is widely regarded as a serious problem for humanity. It's ironic, however, that historically the chief threat posed by global warming is not the warming phase itself. A warming climate leads to more congenial temperatures, enhanced availability of food, and encourages a growing human population. Examples include the Middle Bronze Age (3300 – 1200 BCE), the Roman Warm Period (300 BCE – 400 CE), the Medieval Warm Period (750 – 1250 CE) and the Modern Warm Time (1860 to present). The real problem comes not so much from the warming trend itself but from the human population growth that a warming climate encourages. When a cooling trend arrives, agriculture is inevitably disrupted, leading to famine, epidemics, and the breakdown or outright collapse of human societies.

The real challenge facing humanity today is not so much the rising sea levels, the drying deserts, or ecological disruption caused by global warming. The problem is the explosive increase in human populations that has occurred over the last 150 years of the Modern Warm Time. How sustainable will those populations be when the next cooling trend arrives? At the end of the Medieval Warm Period, the human population on earth was about 400 million people. Now, during the Modern Warm Time, the worldwide population is approaching eight billion people. If agricultural production is substantially interrupted for even a few years, which has happened twice in the last two centuries (the Tambora and Krakatoa eruptions), billions of people will be at risk of starvation.

That's the bad news.

The good news is that, unlike the people of the Late Bronze Age, the end of the Roman Warm Period, or the end of the Medieval Warm Period, we are aware of the danger looming when the next cooling trend arrives. When a Tambora-class volcano explodes sometime in the future, we know the net effect will be a global cooling of between 1°C and 3°C worldwide that can last for up to ten years. Judging by what we learned after the Pinatubo eruption (1991), however, we can expect that the cooling will not be uniform. Some parts of the world will be affected more than others. Agricultural production may decline, but it won't cease almost entirely like it did in Europe in 1257 (eruption of Samalas in Indonesia) or in 1600 (eruption of the Huaynaputina volcano in Peru). Also, in 1257 and 1600 farmers had almost no flexibility to switch from warm-loving crops (rice, wheat, corn) to crops that can handle cooler temperatures (potatoes, turnips, carrots, beets). In the future, farmers will have more options to adjust to cooling temperatures. Finally, if humans can manage a little cooperation following a climate reversal, widespread famine and epidemics can, at least in theory, be avoided.

It is probable that the earliest fully modern *Homo sapiens* living in Africa were almost driven into extinction 73,500 years ago when the Toba volcano exploded in Sumatra and produced a climate reversal that may have lasted for one thousand years. But by that time, proto-humans had already been dealing with climate change for at least four million years. In fact, one can easily argue that, if the climate in East Africa hadn't turned warmer and drier ten million years ago and caused the dense tropical forests to turn into grasslands, humans may never have evolved in the first place. Our species has successfully dealt with countless climate reversals in the past.

We'll have to do it again sometime in the future.

REFERENCES

1. Hart, M.H., 1978. The evolution of the atmosphere of the Earth. Icarus, 33(1), pp.23-39.

www.ingramcontent.com/pod-product-compliance
Lightning Source LLC
Chambersburg PA
CBHW070331090426
42733CB00012B/2443